European Security in the 1990s

Transnational Institute Series

Already published

Forthcoming

European Security
in the 1990s

EDITED AND INTRODUCED BY DAN SMITH

PLUTO PRESS

with the Transnational Institute (TNI)

First published 1989 by Pluto Press
345 Archway Road
London N6 5AA
in association with the Transnational Institute
Paulus Potterstraat 20
1071 DA Amsterdam

Distributed in the USA by Unwin Hyman Inc.
8 Winchester Place, Winchester
MA 01890, USA

Distributed in the Netherlands by the Transnational Institute

Typesetting: Ránsom Electronic Publishing,
Woburn Sands, Bucks

British Library Cataloguing in Publication Data
Smith, Dan, 1951–
    European Security in the 1990s.
    1. Western Europe. International security
    I. Title
    327.1'16

    ISBN 0–7453–0332–3 hb
    ISBN 0–7453–0343–9 pb

Printed and bound in the UK by
Billing & Sons Ltd, Worcester

Contents

About the Authors

Mariano Aguirre is Director of the Peace Research Centre (Centro de Investigación para la Paz) Madrid, and a Fellow of the Transnational Institute. His most recent publication, *The Reagan Doctrine and US Interventionism: The Cases of Nicaragua, Angola and Libya*, is published in Spanish in 1989.

Robert L. Borosage was the Chief Issues Advisor to the Jesse Jackson 1988 US Presidential Election Campaign. He is a Senior Fellow and former Director of the Institute for Policy Studies in Washington DC.

Malcolm Chalmers is a Lecturer in the Department of Peace Studies, University of Bradford, and writes on defence and disarmament issues. His recent publications include *Is There a Tank Gap? Comparing NATO and Warsaw Pact Tank Fleets* (with Lutz Unterseher) and *START and Britain's Nuclear Force*.

Gerard Holden is a Research Officer at the Science Policy Research Unit, University of Sussex, and a Fellow of the Transnational Institute. His *The Warsaw Pact: Soviet Security and Bloc Politics* is published in 1989, and he is co-editor (with Richard Falk and Mary Kaldor) of *The New Detente: Rethinking East–West Relations* (also 1989).

Mario Pianta is a researcher on economics and technology at Italy's National Research Council, Rome. He is the author of *New Technologies Across the Atlantic: US Leadership or European Autonomy?*.

Dan Plesch is Director of BASIC, an independent research and information organisation with offices in London and Washington. The organisation provides an educational and information service on national security issues in and between the US and the UK, with special reference to the NATO alliance, publishing regular reports.

Christiane Rix is a peace researcher at the Hamburg Institute of Peace Research and Security Policy, writing on the security policies and interests of both German states and the GDR's position within the Warsaw

Treaty Organisation. Her most recent piece is on the German question from the point of view of Germany's European neighbours.

Dan Smith is Associate Director of the Transnational Institute and a writer on politico-strategic issues. His most recent publication is *Pressure: How America Runs NATO*. He was Chairperson of END in 1981–2 and Vice-Chairperson of CND from 1984–7.

Introduction:
Changing Times – New Agendas

Discussion in Europe about security, defence and disarmament has involved more people and been more intense in the 1980s than at any other time since 1945. This was evident not only within the mass peace movements, but also in a plethora of publications explaining the nuclear predicament, canvassing ways out of it, developing new concepts for international politics. As a result the debate was not only wider and sharper than before, but also far better informed and more profound.

Set against the many grim features of the 1980s, this combination of political and intellectual activity is worth celebrating. It has subjected the old orthodoxies to incisive critiques and erected new constraints around the plans and policies of armourers and strategists. If it survives, we can start the last decade of this century in the reasonable hope that headway can be made in resolving some of the world's most intractable problems.

We will need a similar combination if we are to turn that hope into reality. The improvement in East–West relations in the second half of the 1980s has generated an atmosphere of optimism. But it has by no means eliminated armed confrontation or the causes of war – even if it has lessened the risk of a major conflagration – and it has only marginally reduced the incidence of wars in the Third World. We still live on an armed and warring planet which houses the potential for annihilation on an unprecedented and unimaginable scale, including the possible extinction of the human race.

The changes that have taken and are still taking place are important, and many of them are for the better. Most notably, far-reaching changes in the USSR have produced new policies which have made possible a series of breakthroughs in East–West relations. In the USA, after riding to power on the crest of anti-Soviet enmity from which he went on to oversee the largest peacetime increase in US military spending, Ronald Reagan ended his term as President as the co-architect of a new US–Soviet detente. This produced the first super-power agreement to reduce nuclear weapons – the Intermediate Nuclear Forces (INF) Treaty – and created the possibility of more arms cuts, both nuclear and conventional.

Yet changes of a different kind are also under way. In the USA the school of military thought which used to be known as 'counter-insurgency warfare' has re-emerged with a new name – Low-Intensity Conflict (LIC). Like its predecessor, it focuses on the use of armed force in Third World conflicts. For several years after the USA's debacle in Vietnam, there were severe political inhibitions against doing anything which looked like leading to a repeat performance. Throughout its eight years the Reagan administration set about breaking these inhibitions. It embarked on some military adventures alone – Grenada and Libya, aid to the *contras* in Nicaragua, use of US advisers in El Salvador. In others – the Lebanon and Persian Gulf – it recruited Western European help. The new emphasis on LIC was a deeply negative development of the 1980s; even worse was the Western European governments' willingness to be drawn along in the USA's wake.

The North Atlantic Treaty defines an area – North America, Europe, the Mediterranean and the Atlantic as far south as the Tropics – within which members are obliged to assist each other in the event of aggression. NATO strategy since its inception has focused on central Europe; today, it is also looking south and south-east. The Mediterranean is no longer just the 'Southern Flank' – it is becoming a second major front in its own right. It is the strategic link between continental Europe and the troubled zones of North Africa and the Middle East. Out of public sight, NATO has developed plans to allow US forces in Europe to be first reserves for military action in the Middle East. Other NATO states would help US forces get out of Europe, replace them and possibly join in US operations. All these plans are directed at operations outside the NATO area.

At the same time as peace movements address these changes, they still have to contend with more familiar problems. With its evident scepticism about detente in early 1989, the Bush administration seems set to turn away from the rosy glow of Dr Feelgood from California's last two years. But it is unlikely to repeat the tone of the early Reagan years. What Bush offers is the old orthodoxy without the heat, confrontation without panic, a new old conservatism. One expression of this approach was the pressure the Bush administration began to put on the European allies, immediately after it took office, to accept a new round of nuclear deployments in Europe.

NATO has not taken any steps away from its strategy of 'flexible response'. Adopted in 1967, this is directed at finding appropriate levels of military response to any kind of aggression. Its central, most dangerous and controversial element is the willingness to use nuclear weapons first: to start a nuclear war. Over the years, numerous critics –

by no means exclusively on the left or from peace movements – have torn the faulty logic of 'flexible response' apart. But NATO remains wedded to it because it is politically important. It is the ultimate binding constituent in the glue which holds NATO together. Since most of the nuclear weapons available to NATO are US-made, 'flexible response' symbolises and ensures Western Europe's strategic dependence on the USA. It is also seen by Western European governments as a guarantee that their security is inextricably linked to the USA's.

Plans have been on the table for several years to update the nuclear arsenal in Europe and take 'flexible response' into the next century. It was on these that the Bush administration's first intra-alliance diplomacy focused in February 1989. At that time, it was far from certain that they could be implemented. Apart from Margaret Thatcher's, most European NATO governments simply did not want to risk provoking peace movements into a new round of mobilisation. But in the end there is much more at stake than domestic political considerations in Western European countries.

As with other items on NATO's agenda – 'out-of-area' operations, the right level of military spending, arms control – three major questions are bound up in the immediate policy issue. One is the East–West relationship. To deploy the new tactical nuclear weapons would signal that NATO has a strictly limited interest in detente, that it is determined not to let the relationship with the USSR change dramatically, that it does not want military confrontation in Europe to be significantly reduced.

The second issue is the continuing but slow process of US decline. Reagan was the evangelist not only of anti-Sovietism but also of American resurgence, yet he ended his presidency amid a more widespread awareness of relative decline than when he began. To resist decline, the Bush administration must – among many other things – assert its leadership of NATO. This it will do in part by trying to get the allies to accept the new nuclear weapons, spend more on the military, follow its lead on arms control and detente and participate in military operations in the Third World.

How Western European governments respond will do much to define their relations with the USSR and the Third World as well as the USA. And it will have further effects. EC market integration by the end of 1992 marks a major milestone on the road to Western European unity. Many think this necessarily means greater independence from the USA, not just in economic affairs but in politics and security as well. Accepting US leadership over strategic issues, as Western Europe has for the past two decades, would limit its political independence. So what is at stake is not simply Western Europe's international relations, but the nature of Western Europe itself.

Detente has given us a glimpse of a better future. Prospects for achieving it are stronger than in the first period of detente in the late 1960s and early 1970s, not least because of changes in the USSR, but also because US decline has continued and Western European unity is less of a pipedream. But the future is far from certain. The further development of detente faces strong resistance in the USA, Britain and the NATO establishment, and Mikhail Gorbachev may not be able to keep making initiatives indefinitely without more positive responses from the West. And detente will be directly affected by US decline, which will continue but at an uncertain pace, and Western European unity, the form and meaning of which are still unclear.

So, one way or another, the overriding theme of the security debate as we enter the 1990s is change. For political action on these questions to be effective, the nature of this change must be clearly understood. That is why we have written this book. The emphasis is on analysing what is happening and what it may lead to. But this consistently leads to sometimes explicit and sometimes implicit proposals for alternatives to current NATO policies, and agendas for political action. Our aim, in fact, has been very ambitious: it is to map out the major issues of European security in the 1990s so that political movements are equipped to deal with them.

We start on the changing strategic context of European security. My own chapter looks at its main features, including the new detente, the West's response and the overall direction of NATO and Soviet policies. Assessing the superpowers is taken further by Bob Borosage on the Bush administration and Gerard Holden on Soviet policy and military doctrine. Perhaps paradoxically, the fact that Soviet leaders have acknowledged the weaknesses of their own system does not mean that the Bush administration's course will be smooth or easy. Indeed, faced with huge deficits in the trade balance and Federal budget, the USA faces severe difficulties as it seeks a way out of decline and tries to secure its world power. Soviet policy seems likely to be more productive for detente than the West's. Profound changes in approach have begun to feed through into military doctrine and deployment, and so far it appears that any opposition to this within the armed forces is being overridden. Conservatism within the USSR, however, is not the major reason for sounding a note of caution. To be fruitful, Gorbachev's initiatives need a positive Western response which is so far non-existent.

Christiane Rix's chapter on the two German states examines the influence of the changing strategic context in central Europe. East and West Germany are together the core area of military confrontation in

Europe and each has a degree of influence in their respective military alliances. How they respond to the changes, therefore, is particularly sensitive. In both states, conservative governments face difficulties in responding to the new climate. In East Germany, the problems are more severe in domestic politics, where the government seeks to outflank pressures for reforms in the Gorbachev mode, by adopting some of his new approach to foreign policy. In West Germany, the Bonn government – caught between conflicting pressures from the electorate and from Washington – faces difficulties in international and security policy, particularly on the issue of the new tactical systems.

The chapters by Malcom Chalmers and Dan Plesch take us from the political and strategic background into immediate policy issues on, respectively, arms control and weapons procurement. Chalmers starts his outline of conventional arms control possibilities by dissecting NATO's long-standing complaints about its inferiority in non-nuclear forces. The evidence of conventional inferiority has never been as clear as the right has made it sound. The likelihood of these military machines going to war will not be reduced simply by marginal cuts in force levels. What is needed is to fit arms control into a concept of a safe framework for European security. Short-term steps which create the conditions for greater mutual trust and confidence are both necessary and feasible, and could pave the way for major reductions in armed forces.

An arms control forum exists for both conventional and strategic nuclear forces, but not for tactical nuclear weapons. NATO wants things to stay that way. Although the in-principle decisions on deploying new tactical nuclear weapons were taken as long ago as 1983 and have been refined since, specific deployment decisions had not been taken by early 1989. Plesch's chapter sets these plans in their NATO context, explaining why the new weapons may be deployed, and why they should not, before setting out a guide to their characteristics and possible numbers which will be a useful reference source.

Mario Pianta addresses the virtually forgotten issue of the late 1980s – Star Wars. Having dominated strategic debate in the USA in the period 1983–6, it is now widely viewed as a dead issue. This is a mite premature. Big business, especially US business, is in too deep. There may be cuts in the programme, but completely eliminating it would be extremely difficult and is very unlikely. Large US military programmes have an extraordinary track record of resilience. Moreover, from its inception, Star Wars has embodied a technological strategy for resisting US decline. It is on this aspect that Pianta focuses. Despite its evident shortcomings, the strategy could give the USA a decisive advantage in the next round of technological competition, but only if Western European states and Japan can be sucked deeply enough into its orbit.

Finally Mariano Aguirre looks south – because that is where NATO's gaze is increasingly cast. The USA's pressure on its European allies to support Third World operations both directly and indirectly is simultaneously a sign of its relative decline and a way of shoring up its leadership by getting the allies to share the costs of its world role. At a time when East–West and trans-Atlantic relations could be reshaped, it is fundamentally misconceived for Western European governments to follow this path which may lead to a revival of European imperialism. Instead, what is needed is to take advantage of present opportunities to develop entirely new ways of conceiving and planning for security, to change the terms of the conception of security itself.

Throughout the book, the three issues of detente, US decline and Western European unity recur. What happens on these fronts will be decisive in shaping the framework of European security. If we are correct in believing that effective political action is built on understanding these issues, and especially the changes in world politics in the late 1980s, a quartet of broad conclusions emerges from the book.

Peace movements must be responsive both to improvements in East–West relations and to the possibility of Cold War tensions resurfacing more strongly if confrontation persists. They need also to see how the interplay of US decline with moves towards Western European unity creates new risks for the Third World; they should prepare to resist the onset of a nascent neo-imperialism in Western Europe. At the same time, that trans-Atlantic interplay creates room for manoeuvre to expand detente policies. And all of this emphasises that the cornerstone of the movements' effectiveness will be their ability to focus national concerns within a transnational perspective. If this book helps meet that challenge, its authors will be well satisfied.

Dan Smith
Brighton, February 1989

1

The Changing Strategic Context

DAN SMITH

The 1980s opened with the end of superpower detente and the beginning of a new Cold War. By the end of the decade the atmosphere had
changed remarkably. Ronald Reagan, elected US President in
November 1980 as the apostle of a stronger and more confrontational
America, ended his second term in office celebrating the gains of a
new detente with the USSR – including the Treaty on Intermediate
Nuclear Forces (INF) signed in December 1987 and ratified the
following May.

In the early 1980s the dangers produced by the combination of arms
race and confrontation provoked a powerful public response. First in
Western Europe, then in the USA and the countries of the Pacific,
mass peace movements became potent political forces. They expressed
the sharp edge of widespread public alarm at the rising dangers. In
different countries each movement had its own idea of the problems
and risks of world politics, but running through the differences there
were common strands. Contrary to orthodox interpretations which see
the threat of nuclear war as a result of the USSR's aggressive ambitions,
which must therefore be resisted everywhere, the movement stressed
that the threat arose from confrontation itself – it was the product of
competitive policies on both sides. Whether or not anybody actually
sought a nuclear war (which seemed unlikely even in the case of the
most strident of hawks) their policies and actions created the risk of
precisely such a disaster.

At their best, the movements not only found imaginative new ways
to oppose the arms race, focusing in Europe on the deployment of
Cruise and Pershing 2 missiles, but they also developed an alternative
to living constantly on the brink of nuclear conflagration. This
rejected the *realpolitik* of strategic balance and confrontation between
rival blocs. The failure of arms control through the 1960s and 1970s
led, to different degrees among the various movements, to the idea of
unilateral disarmament. For some, unilateralism was a moral imperative; for others it was either a means to break the logjam of
negotiations, or it meant simply the overdue abandonment of
weapons and strategies which were both useless and dangerous.

Unilateralism became the basis for an alternative approach founded on the understanding that world security is mutual.

'National security' is in many ways an outmoded and dangerous concept which serves merely to justify confrontation; it has become another word for the pursuit of power. Security should not be about the power interests of states, but about the interests of ordinary people living in reasonable degrees of prosperity, free from the threat of war and environmental disaster, in democracy and a just world order. The peace movements looked for policies which embodied and implemented interdependence by reducing confrontation.

A key part of their approach lay in understanding – often implicitly – that perception can be an important strategic factor. Mutual suspicion and hostility, sustained over decades, blind strategists and politicians to the effects their policies have on the other side. What Washington sees as a defensive measure the Kremlin all too easily views as a threat, and *vice versa*. Reducing confrontation therefore meant adopting policies which provided security without appearing to impose a threat. Policies of common security and strategies of defensive defence were developed in which the absence of aggressive intent would be inescapably evident.[1]

But by the end of the 1980s, having explained the dangers and proposed alternatives, the peace movements face some serious questions. Were the dangers as great as we thought? Were the institutions of armament and confrontation as incapable of controlling the risks as we supposed? Was arms control such a dead letter? With better relations between the USA and the USSR, and with Cruise and Pershing 2 missiles consigned by treaty to the scrap heap, are the alternatives we developed relevant? If it is true that world politics are entering a less perilous phase, who needs peace movements?

Is the Cold War Over?

The problem for the movements is that these questions are not only pertinent – and their answers not always comforting – but they must be addressed in a changing strategic context. Perhaps the most dramatic symbol of change came when Reagan visited Moscow in Spring 1986 for his fourth meeting with Mikhail Gorbachev. Questioned about his description of the USSR as the 'evil empire' in a famous speech in February 1983, he replied that it was no longer relevant. Along with that epithet, he presumably buried all the other anti-Soviet rhetoric that had marked his administration in its first years of power.

This change has prompted numerous commentators to declare that the Cold War is over. On the right some have gone further, evoking a propaganda of triumphalism. They emphasise the elements of *perestroika* in the USSR which seem to accept the superiority of Western ways, especially in economics and commerce; they point with thinly disguised glee at the explosive nationalities problem; and they ignore the rest. At the same time, of course, they are ignoring the failures of capitalism – devastation in the Third World, brutal marginalisation of the poor in developed countries, and the continuing potential for destructive instability in the world economy.

In fact, some voices on the right warn against triumphalism. They fear that Gorbachev's reform programme will work and eventually produce a leaner, fitter USSR – more efficient, more dynamic, better able to compete for world power. Triumphalism, they argue, is premature.

Shallow as the triumphalist calls are, they should not be dismissed. If the Cold War is seen as a conflict between two necessarily competing social and economic systems, it can be argued that the Soviet leadership in the 1980s has implicitly conceded defeat. The criticisms of the Soviet system made by Gorbachev and his senior colleagues cannot convincingly be reconciled with a continued claim that it is a model for other societies to follow. If Soviet socialism produces shoddy goods, widespread shortages, corruption, nepotism, rampant alcoholism, a 20 per cent loss of each year's harvest because of inefficient transport and storage, economic stagnation, a stolid and inefficient bureaucracy, an alienated population – if this has been the Soviet system according to its leaders, where then is the claim to superiority?

Of course, any such critique should not lose sight of one of the Soviet system's strengths. It has engendered the potential for its own reform, and in so doing has swept away the Western conservatives' argument that it could not reform itself. *Perestroika* has not been imposed from the outside. It is not the product of any Western intervention.

But with or without the triumphalism, claims that the Cold War is over beg the question, what is (or was) it about? Seen as a fundamental conflict between different and necessarily competing social systems, it is not over. The goal of *perestroika* is not capitalism. It is distinctly a project to renovate socialism. If Soviet socialism is not going to transmogrify into advanced capitalism – and with no sign of *vice versa* being on the cards – the difference between the two systems will not be eliminated. But in fact those differences do not go very far towards explaining the Cold War. Accommodation between the USA and the People's Republic of China in the 1970s suggests that differences between social systems need not of themselves cause that sort of conflict. The key point about the Cold War has always been rivalry for world power between the USA and the USSR. Deciding whether it is over means asking if the rivalry has ended, and the answer depends in part how the term 'Cold War' is used.

This does not conclude the basic definition, for there is another point: what is the chronology of the Cold War? Here, with apologies, we enter an issue which may seem purely semantic but is none the less important.

There are two schools of thought. One uses the term 'Cold War' to describe the whole fabric of US–Soviet relations since 1945; the other refers by it to two specific periods.[2] I am of the second school, largely because it makes it possible to distinguish between different phases of US–Soviet relations. Not to do so means ignoring the possibility of improvements when times are bad and likewise ignoring the possibility of deterioration when times are good.

The two periods described by the second school as Cold War are from shortly after the end of Second World War (there is room for dispute over precise dating) until about 1954–5, and from December 1979, the month NATO announced it would deploy Cruise and Pershing 2 missiles and the USSR invaded Afghanistan. In between came first a series of oscillating relations which included several low points, not least successive Berlin confrontations and the 1962 Cuban missile crisis. Then from the mid-1960s was a period of detente. Both periods saw real improvements and changes in US–Soviet relations, but neither eradicated the fundamental confrontation based on rivalry for power and influence.

These definitional issues profoundly affect the reading of current politics. If 'Cold War' means 'the nature of US–Soviet relations since 1945', a claim that these have taken a profoundly new turn and that the Cold War is therefore over is very sweeping. It implies that either the USA or the USSR no longer seeks to advance its power and influence at the expense of the other and will not protect its sphere from the incursions of the other. At least one superpower must be assumed to have quit – or be on the point of quitting – the world arena. If 'Cold War' describes 'the nature of US–Soviet relations since December 1979', a claim that it is over is far less sweeping. It simply means that – as in the 1970s – the rivalry will be conducted less intensely, with less heated rhetoric, perhaps more cheaply and with less perceived danger of nuclear war. It does not mean that the underlying confrontation has ended.

Only in this second, restricted sense, is it possible to argue that the Cold War is over. Even then, at this time, the argument must be cautious. The beginning of the end of the second Cold War came with the 1985 Geneva summit between Gorbachev and Reagan. The progress registered then was followed up in 1987 with the INF Treaty. But the apparatus of confrontation remains. George Bush has quietly distanced himself from some aspects of the new detente. There is no guarantee that the improvement will endure. If it is to, it will need to take in its stride strategic arms reductions and conventional arms cuts in Europe. These cuts may turn out to be extremely complex tasks – not just technically but politically. Difficulties in completing them may lead to accusations on either side of obstructiveness and malign intent, or simply a loss of momentum which could begin to slide back into a third Cold War period later in the 1990s.

East–West confrontation is about more than the arms race and it ranges wider than Europe. Gorbachev has shown a willingness to restrict Soviet activities in the Third World – for example, withdrawing Soviet troops from Afghanistan and supporting a negotiated settlement between Angola and South Africa to permit the withdrawal of Cuban troops. Numerous commentators on Soviet politics report that there is now less interest than before in taking sides in Third World conflicts – because the dividends have not usually been very great. But the USSR remains a world power, with allies and interests from Cuba to South-east Asia, in Africa and the Middle East; and the USA shows no sign of intending to be less energetic in the Third World.

Though the changes which have occurred are important, and though they could and should be the harbinger of more, a return to Cold War is possible. The momentum is in the right direction, but it could be reversed. In that grim case, the late 1980s would appear as a breathing space filled with lost opportunities, not a decisive break.

The Threat to Security

In the early 1980s the peace movements saw a real threat of nuclear war. Its source lay in the dramatic deterioration in East–West relations and the intensity of confrontation, the apocalyptic and militantly evangelical anti-Soviet tone of the Reagan administration, combined with the arms race, strategies for selective use of nuclear weapons and too much flirtation with the idea of winning a nuclear war. The movements alerted public opinion to both the threat and the need to resist it.

But if the threat is a product of confrontation, improved US–Soviet relations diminish it. Awareness of that may be difficult for movements which tend to thrive most when people are most anxious about nuclear war and determined to do something about it. But it is clearly essential to acknowledge it, or movements will simply moan along on the margins of politics, weaken themselves and be unable to resist the threats to security which persist despite better US–Soviet relations.

In fact, even in the worst period of the Cold War in the 1980s the threat of nuclear conflagration was not as great as some activists argued. In 1983 there were people who said that once Cruise missiles were deployed at Greenham Common the base would be attacked by the USSR. Others focused on the Pershing 2 missiles deployed in the Federal Republic of Germany which, because of their very short flight-time to targets in the USSR, were rightly seen as particularly dangerous. Again, arguments were heard that deploying Pershing 2s would give the USSR no choice but to launch a nuclear attack.

These were wild exaggerations, in their own way just as feverish as many of the wilder things said by the Reaganites. They ignored the obvious stupidity of such a nuclear strike. The resulting war would destroy the USSR. They assumed the worst of the Soviet leadership, in a manner not very different from the 'worst-case' analyses of Western hawks.

The shortcomings of deterrence theory and strategy do not reside at the level of rational calculation. Any US or Soviet leadership which has time to think clearly will, if it even gets as far as contemplating a surprise nuclear strike, turn down the option because of the consequences. The problem is that a crisis may leave little or no time to think, or create an atmosphere of hostile panic which precludes clear thinking. Coming out of a period of intense confrontation, with a background of hostility, non-communication and the tendency to think the worst of each other, such a crisis could be extremely dangerous. It is then that the supreme irrationality of launching a nuclear war could come to be seen as the only option. The crackpot logic of US hawks in the early 1980s made such an outcome to a major crisis seem more than possible.

Such a crisis seems less likely at the end of the 1980s than it used to. It is not impossible, but it is a threat which has diminished. But it could also grow. If the immediate dangers appear to have receded, the durability of confrontation could, despite current hopes, bring them flooding back.

This gives an answer to the question about who needs the peace movements. Their task is not complete, and will not be until and unless confrontation becomes not just less dangerous, but non-existent. Until then, we shall always need movements able to challenge the policies and philosophy of confrontation, resist the armourers' plans, and promote different modes for international relations and new concepts of security. The aim must be to help an improving situation improve further.

The 'Gorbachev Challenge'

It has been clear since early 1987 that Gorbachev seeks a profound restructuring of international relations. Soviet foreign policy has been unhitched from the conventions of the Brezhnev years and before. The new keynote is not international class conflict, but international interdependence. The shift derives from a recognition in the USSR that nuclear war would be a global disaster in which notions of victory would be meaningless, and also that the Soviet Union has multiple links with the world economy and political community.[3] It does not mean the end of the USSR's status as a great power but it does necessitate basic changes in policy. The result has been a series of ever bolder and more imaginative initiatives. Together with a widespread desire in NATO countries for the consequent opportunities to be taken up, these constitute a major element in the changing strategic context – the 'Gorbachev challenge'.

What is not clear is how far *perestroika* in Soviet foreign policy is intended to go – much less, how far it can go, since that also depends on Western responses. In particular, it is unclear how far it will go in Europe. *Perestroika* is clearly partly an attempt to cut the costs of the Eastern European *cordon sanitaire* constructed by Stalin. That means arms reductions, certainly, but could it go as far as complete military withdrawal – at least from Hungary and Czechoslovakia? It is also unclear how the Soviet leadership would react if such withdrawal released explosive pressures for reform in those countries – or if the lid were to blow off because withdrawal was incomplete. Has the Brezhnev doctrine of limited sovereignty, which was used to justify the blighting of the 1968 Prague Spring, been completely jettisoned, or is there life in it yet?

These unanswered questions – perhaps unanswerable except in the event – suggest it would be wrong to identify wholly with Gorbachev's foreign policy, and especially to read into it motives which may not exist. But that reservation should not detract from recognising that as things stand at the end of the 1980s, the obstacle to further improvement in international politics is NATO's allegiance to the same basic assumptions that have guided it for 40 years.

In 1988 Professor Michael Howard – who in 1980 was the target of E.P. Thompson's polemic, *Protest and Survive*[4] – wrote an article discussing NATO's response to the Gorbachev challenge. He outlined the alliance's policy options in terms of four models. Model A stood for Apocalypse (the USSR disintegrates). In B for Benign, a calm and secure USSR reaches accommodation with Europe and there are major arms reductions. In C for Confrontation, the *status quo* is preserved. In

D for Disaster or Domination, the USSR conquers Western Europe.[5]

The USSR's disintegration is the dream of the US right but, as Howard argues, in the unlikely event that it happened its results could be as destructive for the West as for the USSR. A significant spectrum of opinion both in the USA and Western Europe now seeks an accommodation in Europe. But others fear that behind the new benign appearance, the USSR's long-term ambitions have only been put on hold. At the end of the day that leaner, fitter USSR will emerge and we will have Model D – Soviet domination. For fear of that, NATO leaders will distrust the attractions of Model B and opt for Model C.

This, Howard argues, may be the short-term necessity from a NATO perspective, but it is not satisfactory in the longer run. The very cautiousness which makes it attractive to NATO leaders makes it unattractive to a growing constituency in Western Europe which wants a bolder, more forward-looking response to the Gorbachev challenge.

But C stands not just for Confrontation; it is also for Convenient – continuing confrontation involves the least change for NATO. For an alliance of considerable complexity in which strategic policies are set by political compromise, options which offer the least change are the most attractive. Further, as Howard points out, if Model B for Benign were followed, NATO's very existence would come into question: 'With a Soviet Union generally friendly and cooperative, would there be any further need for it?' What this points to, without quite reaching, is that the NATO states have their own need for confrontation. That Gorbachev's Soviet Union is a challenge for NATO – rather than an opportunity – is precisely the problem with it.

Howard neatly describes NATO's difficulties:

> Gorbachev's technique is now clear. It is to ask us to state our demands and then simply to meet them. We demanded that the Soviet Union should leave Afghanistan. He has done so. We demanded that he should scrap the SS-20s and their smaller adjuncts. He did it. We demanded that such scrapping should be verified by intrusive on-site inspection. He agreed. We demanded that troop-reductions in Europe should be asymmetrical. He has agreed to that as well. We demanded that the offensive development and training of Soviet forces in Eastern Europe should be abandoned for an overtly defensive posture. He has made his military re-examine their doctrine. What can one do with such a man?

While this overstates the influence of external demands and pressure on Soviet policy, the drift of the argument is absolutely right, encapsulated in the tongue-in-cheek exasperation of the last sentence. Gorbachev is not a blessing for NATO.

Advocates of continuing confrontation buttress their preference with the view that Gorbachev's policies are just a smokescreen to deceive the West into lowering its guard. There was a time in the 1960s when US conservatives viewed the Sino–Soviet split as the same sort of monumental charade. This is false comfort; as Howard says, 'To make matters worse, Gorbachev probably means all that he says'. Greater comfort for confrontationists may be found in the thought that although Gorbachev is sincere, he is unlikely to get his way with policies that hurt the sectional interests of the Soviet military. This is why Gorbachev's United Nations speech in December 1988 was a source of discomfort. The unilateral military reductions he announced then were significant in themselves – troop-cuts of half a million, including 50,000 soldiers and 5,000 tanks from Czechoslovakia, East Germany and Hungary; another 5,000 tanks from the western USSR, 8,500 artillery pieces and 800 combat aircraft; plus unspecified cuts in Asian USSR and Mongolia.[6] But they were more important as a sign that Gorbachev was not only sincere but could also still get his own way.

So what can NATO do? Howard provides two versions of the answer. Since he was previously the object of an attack about whose venom he had reasonable grounds for complaint, for he was not the advocate of Cruise missiles and war-fighting strategies Thompson took him for, I should repeat that he regards the answer as inadequate. In the first version, NATO can, he says:

> take no risks, continue to maintain and improve our existing level of defences (including strategic defences), work cautiously at the margins for incremental confidence-building measures of arms control, and in general proceed on the assumption that no fundamental changes are occurring in the Soviet Union, none can be expected, and even if they did they would make no difference.

The second version is more activist:

> We must conduct a skilful delaying campaign in the certain knowledge that we have powerful allies in the enemy camp. We must block Gorbachev's radical proposals, or counter them with demands for radical troop cuts and redeployments of Soviet armed forces which, however attractive to Gorbachev himself, will be quite unacceptable to his military leadership and their political allies. Together with them, sooner or later, we can wear the man down and frustrate his disturbing designs: after that it may be another generation before

a Soviet leader emerges with the energy to try again. All that is required is patience and the negotiating skills at which the Alliance is now so adept.

In this version, for NATO to sit tight and do little or nothing is not simply to hope that Gorbachev will go away – it is to try to hasten the day when he does.

The strategy may be misconceived, for the 'allies in the enemy camp' on whom it depends may be less powerful than it supposes. Western commentators have been expecting Gorbachev to fall flat on his face almost since the minute he took office. So far he has failed to oblige. If NATO pursues this strategy without wearing Gorbachev down, the result will be increasing impatience with its needless obduracy. NATO could then face an even greater crisis of legitimacy than it faced in the first half of the 1980s. But this does seem to be the strategy NATO is following.

The INF Treaty and Beyond

The Treaty on Intermediate Nuclear Forces got rid of land-based nuclear missiles with ranges of between 500 and 5,500 kilometres. It was the first concrete sign of the changing strategic context, the first major achievement of the Gorbachev approach. The number of nuclear weapons it removes is relatively small – 3 or 4 per cent of the world total – but it was the nuclear age's first agreed measure of nuclear disarmament, the first step on a long road.

Advocates of the decision to deploy Cruise and Pershing 2 missiles argue that the Treaty vindicated NATO's policy, and depict it as the product of Western strength and unity. They point out that when the deployment decision was announced in December 1979, it was part of a package which included arms control. The elimination of land-based intermediate-range missiles – the zero option – was taken up by the Reagan administration in October 1981. But its role was not to remove the weapons; rather, it was to facilitate their deployment. It was designed to take the wind from the peace movements' sails by proposing a deal that they would have to support. The movements saw it as a propaganda ploy and were unconvinced. They were right. General Rogers, then NATO's Supreme Allied Commander Europe, said in 1987, 'The truth is that in 1979 some people agreed to a zero option proposal because they thought it would never be accepted by the Soviet Union,'[7] Or as Reagan once said, 'It's not propaganda. It's public relations.'[8]

The Treaty NATO had proposed but did not want was made possible by a combination of three factors. First, Gorbachev wanted it for two reasons. It was desirable in itself as a way of ending the Cold War. Because of a change in Soviet foreign policy, this was seen as a prime objective. There was also an economic motivation: though the Treaty alone will not do much to release resources from the military to the civilian economy in the USSR, it could pave the way to further disarmament agreements from which a much-needed economic bonus could be gained.

The second factor was Western weakness. The Iran–Contragate scandal surfaced in the last few months of 1986 and severely debilitated the US administration. It needed a major foreign policy success to bolster its leadership in NATO and restore credibility at home, and the INF Treaty fitted the bill. Indeed, once Gorbachev announced his support for an INF Treaty in February 1987, the Reagan administration had almost no choice but to go ahead with it.

Public opinion in Western Europe was the third factor. This encouraged Margaret Thatcher (with an election in the offing) to overcome her initial caution. It also shifted West Germany's Chancellor Helmut Kohl out of his more obdurate position. So the peace movements have a share in the credit for the Treaty. They had created the climate in which politicians had to operate.

In all this, Western strength was neither here nor there. To insist that it was decisive, as NATO, governments like Britain's and the ranks of orthodox strategic commentators all do, only reveals the lack of any new thinking in official Western circles with which to respond to the new thinking in the USSR.

NATO's post-INF policy consists of a mix of arms control and rearmament, as follows: supporting US participation in the Strategic Arms Reduction Talks (START) with the USSR; talks on conventional arms control in Europe with the Warsaw Pact; circumventing the INF Treaty with new weapons systems officially described as 'buttressing measures', 'force adjustments', and so forth; reducing the short-range (below 500 km) nuclear inventory and replacing parts of it with new and more effective systems. In short, the policy is business as usual (see Chapter 6).

The INF Treaty has improved the atmosphere for both START and conventional arms talks. The former are usually described as being about halving the US and Soviet strategic nuclear force levels. Because of the odd way weapons are counted – every warhead on a missile counts as one, but a planeload of bombs also counts as one – a treaty on the lines currently being negotiated would actually produce cuts of about one-third. If achieved, which is not certain and may take time, this would be a major reduction, cutting strategic forces to mid-1970s levels. It would not end the arms race or nuclear confrontation, but it would be another step in the right direction. It is acceptable to NATO and the USA partly because it would reduce US spending on strategic forces, partly because the search for nuclear superiority through increased numbers of more accurate weapons has been effectively called off.

The Conference on Armed Forces in Europe (CAFE), which deals with European-based non-nuclear weapons, replaces the negotiations on conventional arms reductions in central Europe which the two blocs opened in 1973. Prospects for agreement are better than before, largely because of the political environment and partly because by covering all of Europe CAFE has a framework which makes more sense (but see Chapter 5 for a closer analysis of the chance of success). NATO's initial negotiating position seeks disproportionate cuts – much larger on the Warsaw Pact side which the USSR has stated it will accept, though how far it will go in disproportionality is not yet clear. The larger the cuts by the Warsaw Pact, the more they will meet NATO's long-standing complaint about its inferiority in conventional forces.

Both START and CAFE would produce agreements advantageous to NATO, though not in the sense of being disadvantageous to the USSR. They would also be desirable in themselves. However, positive developments in arms control are not the whole of NATO's policy.

Discussion of measures to 'compensate' for the INF Treaty began even before it was signed, though the alliance found difficulty in timing their implementation. By the end of 1988 the deployment of new F-111 bombers to Britain had not been formally announced, but for 18 months the plan to do it had been semi-public knowledge. Preparations for the introduction of new short-range nuclear weapons go further back; once the decision to deploy Cruise and Pershing 2 was announced, work immediately started on this element of the arsenal. The first in-principle decision was announced in 1983. It combined net reductions with new weapons. In 1988 NATO put together a new package to reduce nuclear artillery and increase the firepower of short-range missiles. The net result would again be lower numbers. But there was difficulty in deciding when to take the decision formally. Although the tactical nuclear arsenal would be lower than at any time since the late 1950s, NATO officials and defence ministries are well aware that the new weapons will not be popular. As with measures to circumvent the INF Treaty, they are chary of actions which would provoke a new resurgence by the peace movements.

This caution in NATO is a further answer to the question about who needs the peace movements. Even at lower levels of political activity and numerical strength than in the early 1980s, they are potent political forces. Thatcher, of course, would prefer to ignore that and steam ahead with new deployments. Other Western European leaders are less convinced that they can get away with it and in 1988 the Reagan administration was prepared to listen to their objections – purely tactical and temporary, they assured him – to going ahead quickly.

Atlanticism

The question must arise, why does NATO have such difficulty facing up to the Gorbachev challenge? Why does it cling to old strategic assumptions in changing strategic circumstances?

The official answer is of course that the USSR is not, or may not be, as benign as it appears under Gorbachev – or if it is that it may not remain so for very long. It is an answer produced by unchanging assumptions. It creates a strategy intended to make it into a self-fulfilling prophecy.

But the Soviet threat, which is the basic Western justification for continued confrontation, is a great deal less real than is pretended. With Gorbachev in power the argument that the USSR would occupy Western Europe if it wasn't for NATO is increasingly hard to sustain; in the eyes of growing numbers of people, the 'evil emperor' has no clothes – not threatening ones, anyway. But the argument has always been tenuous. The USSR has long been a *status quo* power in Europe, which showed no interest in conquering the Western countries. Military confrontation has been useful in legitimising its garrisoning of Eastern Europe and bringing together a coherent Soviet bloc – but not as a prelude to conquest. In the first Cold War, the USSR made no moves against territory it accepted was within the Western sphere, except for West Berlin in 1948–9. Even then, Stalin was clearly determined to make a show of force rather than actually use it, or he would have ordered the shooting down of Western aircraft which broke the blockade. The offensive doctrines and deployments of Soviet forces in Eastern Europe with heavy concentrations of armoured divisions – something Gorbachev has announced will be changed to clearly defensive deployment – have reflected military doctrines, not political intentions.

In any case, while NATO has consistently bemoaned its conventional military inferiority in Europe, there have always been grounds to doubt the truth of these complaints. Numerical advantage does not necessarily translate into actual superiority. Analyses in the Pentagon in the 1960s found that previous assessments of the European military balance were grossly distorted and concluded that the situation was reasonably satisfactory.[9] Likewise in the 1970s the Pentagon found a rough balance, not the overwhelming Soviet advantage so routinely depicted.[10] Even in the 1980s Pentagon assessments have concluded that NATO forces are adequate to their tasks.[11] In 1987, the Deputy Supreme Allied Commander Europe was quoted as saying, 'We could handle a five-to-one Soviet superiority.'[12] Nobody has ever depicted the Warsaw Pact's numerical advantage at that level.

If the military balance is not as bad and the USSR not as malign as is made out, what is NATO's problem with Gorbachev? Why are his policies a challenge rather than an opportunity to wind down an expensive and dangerous confrontation in Europe? The official answer simply repeddles the old orthodoxy, which is now wearing increasingly thin. The real problem is that NATO is an essential part of the framework of Western European politics. What threatens the justification of its existence is seen to threaten that framework.

As a political entity, Western Europe was created in the late 1940s in the aftermath of Second World War. Before then, the idea of a community of interests between the states of what is now Western Europe would have been close to laughable. Between the people, perhaps, on the basis of a humanist or socialist internationalism, but not between the governments of Britain, France, Germany (which was also central European) and Italy. These were imperial rivals. The Second World War ended the great European empires (though the death-throes of the British and French empires continue even into the 1980s) and closed the European age of history. It split Germany, weakened France, finished Italy as a regional power and marked a decisive point in Britain's decline as a world power.

Modern Western Europe was created by Marshall Aid and the formation of NATO in 1947–8 and 1948–9 respectively. Both were US projects, reconstructing the economies of Western Europe and providing a stable political framework. The Western European states requested economic assistance, but it was George Marshall, the US Secretary of State, who told them what kind of aid programme to seek. The US administration insisted on a coordinated Western European recovery programme – rather than a series of separate national efforts – the progress of which it would monitor closely. British Foreign Secretary Ernest Bevin took the initiative in paving the way towards NATO, but he first cleared it with Marshall, and the proposal was then redefined to conform with US preferences before it was publicised.[13]

So it was under US tutelage that Western Europe first experienced a taste of the unity that is now well established as the goal of European Community enthusiasts. The USA was Western Europe's midwife. Economic and political dependence has been eroded since the 1940s.

But in the strategic field, Western European states except France (and there the exemption is not as complete as Charles de Gaulle hoped in the 1960s) remain dependent on the USA. Their security policies are predicated on US capabilities and commitments. This has not prevented disputes over major issues ranging from energy, trade and macro-economic policy to questions like the Middle East, but it has given the USA marked influence over its allies' priorities.

Accepting the primacy of the USA in Western European security is the corner-stone of Atlanticism. Over the years, it has gone beyond a policy and a strategic doctrine to become a philosophy. The impoverished response to Gorbachev makes clear that it has now gone beyond a philosophy to become a habit, an addiction – not just strategic dependence but dependency. And the addicts do not want to give it up.

Lower degrees of confrontation and a path which leads to the eventual dissolution of the blocs may create greater possibilities for freedom in Eastern Europe. This is one of the Soviet conservatives' fears about Gorbachev's reform programme – and even more do Eastern European conservatives fear it. But it is not only Eastern Europe that will be affected. An open, bold, positive, forward-looking response to Gorbachev's initiatives risks, as far as NATO is concerned, unravelling the modern political framework of Western Europe. It would undermine the case for continued strategic dependence on the USA and create a case for a new Western Europe.

US Decline

The changing strategic context is not only a product of Soviet policy. It also comes from the continuing relative decline of the USA.

It is one of the ironies of the Reagan era that an administration which arrived in Washington determined to restore the USA's world power at all costs – having got into power partly by exaggerating its decline, especially in relation to the USSR, and misidentifying its causes – should reach the end of its term with a feeling of decline so strong in the USA that it is almost palpable.

This creates great difficulties in US political culture. To acknowledge decline, except to blame it on the existing administration and promise that it will be speedily reversed, is extremely difficult for any mainstream politician. Because of that, US politics produce few new analyses of any merit about its real causes and meaning.

The problem is that the USA's relative decline is not the product of the failures of any one administration. At the heart of it lies what Paul Kennedy calls 'overstretch', an inability to provide the resources with which to sustain the panoply of a globally committed power – a condition he sees in all great empires as they enter their waning period.[14] The USA has experienced slower growth in national income and productivity than most of its commercial competitors since the early 1950s. This is steadily piling up difficulties in maintaining its global military apparatus of more than 500,000 military personnel overseas, over 300,000 of them in and around Europe. As this pressure builds, the need arises to make choices between existing military commitments. But drawing down commitments in any part of the world risks losing power and influence there. The hallmark of the Reagan administration was to deny the need for, or the possibility of, making such choices. Everything – and more of it – was necessary in the USA's biggest military spending boom outside times of major war.

Decline is not purely economic. The defeat in Vietnam was an enormous strategic blow, not only in itself, but also because it created the 'Vietnam syndrome' – deep public reluctance to committing forces overseas in combat. This is a terrible weakness for a great power, which may have many other instruments of power – not least the world financial system via the International Monetary Fund and World Bank – but which needs to be able to use direct means when indirect ones fail. The Reagan administration committed itself against the Vietnam Syndrome; it invaded Grenada, bombed Libya, put forces into Lebanon and ships into the Persian Gulf. Yet the syndrome remained strong, with majority opinion clearly against any use of force which could lead to protracted war.

Politically, the USA's grip on its major allies has also weakened compared with the 1950s – though here through NATO in Europe and the Cold War the Reagan administration did manage to restore some of the influence lost under its predecessors. But that was influence over governments. The USA's political and ideological attractiveness to public opinion has clearly fallen over the years. In the long term this may be the most important factor; it must inevitably reduce support for continued strategic dependence and participation in a US-led alliance.

The USA's decline is real, but it is also relative and slow. The US remains the leading world power. There is as yet no power vacuum waiting to be filled. In these circumstances US administrations into the next century have two options. They can choose to manage decline gracefully, accepting that in historic perspective it is inevitable, and committing themselves to ensuring that it happens without cataclysms along the way. Or they can resist it, shoring up positions of advantage where they can, grabbing new ones where possible, adjusting to circumstances only if there is no alternative.

Decline, no matter how graceful and well managed, does not bring in votes. US political culture dictates that no President and few other politicians will choose the first option – not openly, at least. Of course, things may change in the next decade, especially if the Federal deficit hits the 1990s economy hard. But the second option is far more likely.

To resist decline is difficult and complex. It requires a series of deft balancing acts. The task will be all the harder if clear choices are not made between priorities, and US overseas military commitments are not cut. But it is not beyond the reach of the Bush administration and its successors. For all its bravado and rhetoric, the Reagan administration proved adept at making tactical adjustments to both policy and its presentation to ease its own preferences past allied governments' resistance. The first and most notable example of this was its adoption of arms control on INF in 1981, only months after arriving in power foreswearing arms control itself. When the need arose the administration was unafraid to use intimidation – for instance, in its resistance to the Greek government's desire to remove US bases. In all of this the USA's job was made easier by the Atlanticism of its European allies, which despite the battering it received from public opinion throughout the 1980s remained strong enough to make them vulnerable to US pressure.

Budgetary Pressures

Reagan's military spending boom was stopped by Congress in the last three years of his administration. There is now general agreement that arms spending has to come down, but little consensus between the important players about what should be cut.

Although arms control may provide some possibilities for cutting expenditure, these should not be overstated. Successful Strategic Arms Reduction Talks could result in large savings. But it would be no surprise if START took some years to produce a treaty and the main savings would not be immediate; they would come further down the line in later reductions in strategic nuclear development and production. In CAFE, NATO's main negotiating position requires such disproportionate cuts that it is hard to see more than three or four divisions being removed from Western Europe. This would not mean large US savings even if NATO's cuts only involved US forces, which is not inevitable. And it would *only* provide savings if the US divisions were not simply removed but demobilised; relocating them back home in new bases (the full costs of which would have to be met by the USA alone) would be more expensive than leaving them where they are.

Unless the USA makes major changes in the way it runs its military effort – including cutting overseas forces – any budgetary savings from arms control are likely to be washed away. The US military system generates permanent pressure for higher spending. This is partly a result of its emphasis on constant technological advance. It also stems from various well-documented habits of the military-industrial complex: underbidding to buy into a contract in the knowledge that later cost overruns will be covered; overcharging for small items; 'gold-plating' cheap and simple weapons systems so they end up expensive and complex; and straightforward corruption.

And there are other pressures. The 1980s saw a return to favour of a school of thought once known as 'counter-insurgency'. Its new name is Low-Intensity Conflict (LIC). In the terminology of the Reagan administration, the highest level of conflict is a major East–West war; the middle level is a major regional war, like that between Iran and Iraq. LIC is the use of armed force below this level. It appears to cover more or less everything from bombing Libya, invading Grenada and sending warships to the Gulf through helping anti-communist governments and insurgents, to military action to end US drug imports. It emphasises the swift use of armed force in the Third World, with precise and limited objectives but with overwhelming power.

The main instruments of LIC are the Special Operations Forces. Spending on them increased from $441 million in 1981 to $2.8 billion budgeted in 1988. In the eight years from 1981 to 1988, the Reagan administration spent a total $9 billion on them; for the next four years to 1992 its plans involved spending the same sum in half the time. These elite forces are backed by what used to be called the Rapid Deployment Force; under Reagan it became the Central Command for Southwest Asia with 200,000 troops at its disposal. And in 1985 the first of five light infantry divisions was formed, specially designed for LIC.

For advocates of LIC the US Army's focus on Europe means it is preparing for the wrong war.[15] The exposition of this view is best known in Western Europe in *Discriminate Deterrence*, the January 1988 report of the Commission on Integrated Long-Term Strategy, a high-powered panel established by the US Departments of Defense and State.[16] It argues that the scenarios of Soviet aggression in Europe or directly against the USA that currently dominate US strategy are 'extreme', and that they distract attention and divert resources from more pressing problems in the Third World, where US military power could and should be used.

The Atlanticists in Western Europe fear that US forces will be withdrawn to make them available for Third World contingencies. In fact, US forces in Europe are already available for Third World actions, and plans have been developed to help their passage and cope with their absence. Whatever happens to US forces in Europe, if more money is spent on the US military apparatus in the Third World, US spending on European-based forces will come into question.

The difficulty for the USA is that if it does withdraw enough forces from Western Europe to ease some of its budgetary problems, it would risk losing influence. The Bush administration's motivation to avoid this may be all the stronger because of fears that European Community economic integration by the end of 1992 will strengthen the development of a major rival trading bloc and harden its attitude in trade negotiations. On the one hand, US pressure through NATO may be one way of limiting the damage to US interests, and the administration will not want to lose that card. On the other, if US troops are withdrawn, Western European resentment may spill over into trade negotiations.

This is the sort of balancing act needed to resist decline. On one side, budgetary pressures and military requirements outside Europe both mean spending less on US forces in Europe; on the other, the need to retain influence in Western Europe militates against such cuts. As we have seen, arms control does not give the USA much help in retaining its balance.

Sharing the Burden

The developing US response to this dilemma may involve some small cuts in military commitments, but its main theme is an attempt to keep the commitments while redistributing the costs. It is a two-pronged strategy.

Ever since NATO was formed, one influential strand of US opinion has suspected the allies of taking a free ride. US forces in Europe have been depicted as generously providing the defence that Western Europeans are either too short-sighted or too cunning to pay for. Intermittent efforts have been made to get the European allies to spend more on the military. They have only ever been partially successful. The foreign and defence ministers have always been willing to sign communiques endorsing increased military spending; they have then usually done nothing about it.

The latest effort came in 1988 under heavy congressional pressure for either increased military spending by the allies, or a greater contribution to the cost of basing US forces in Europe, or both. The term used in Congress is 'burden-sharing'. The idea is that the allies should share more of the burden of their own defence. It is aimed at Japan as well as at Western Europe; both areas are prosperous allies which spend a smaller proportion of their wealth on the military than does the USA, and Congress wants them to spend more. Because it is a tune which has been played so many times before, most Western European governments are rather bored by it. In May 1988 they committed themselves to looking at the problem – but no more. Boosting military spending is unpopular in Western Europe. Even if the NATO governments wanted to go along with burden-sharing, they could find themselves economically and politically unable to oblige the USA. The Bush administration's prospects on this front are far from rosy, though Congress will probably continue to worry at the issue.

There is a hidden logic in burden-sharing. The ostensible case is weak. The USA's forces in Europe support its interests; their presence is not an act of altruism and it is a simple-minded fallacy to pretend it is. Advocates of burden-sharing also paint a misleading picture of the Western European states' military strength. They provide 90 per cent of NATO's manpower and artillery in Europe, 80 per cent of tanks and combat aircraft and 65 per cent of warships. They have 3.5 million people on active duty in the armed forces and the same number in the reserves – compared with the USA's figures of 2.3 million and 1.5 million.[17] Western Europe is hardly unmilitarised; the burden is already being shared. US allies spend less of their wealth on the military than does the USA, but that is hardly surprising. They are regional powers at most, while the USA is a world power with the military apparatus to match.

With the burden-sharing argument the USA is trying to reduce the cost of being NATO's dominant member without sacrificing the benefits. The burden to be shared is the regional element of what the USA pays to be a world power. That logic is even clearer in the second prong of the strategy.

The North Atlantic Treaty has a limited territorial scope – North America, Europe, the Atlantic as far south as the Tropics and the Mediterranean. That is the NATO area. During the 1970s the USA trailed the coat of involvement in 'out-of-area' operations before the allies. Following the fall of the Shah in Iran in 1978 and the 1979 Soviet invasion of Afghanistan the idea took on more impetus and urgency. In his last report as President Carter's Defense Secretary, Harold Brown called for some NATO allies 'to participate directly with us in Southwest Asian defense'.[18] In 1986 Caspar Weinberger, US Defense Secretary during most of the Reagan administration, described the limits on NATO's area as an 'outworn geographical tag'.[19]

The Reagan administration's most notable victory over its allies' reluctance to get involved 'out of area' was in 1987 when warships from Britain, France, Belgium, the Netherlands and Italy joined the US

Navy in policing the Persian Gulf. But this was not done under the aegis of NATO; it was the Western European Union which provided the appropriate call from an international forum.

If the Bush administration succeeds on both these fronts – improbably getting the NATO allies to spend more in Europe either to meet the costs of US forces there or to strengthen their own forces, plus getting them to provide military support for US policy in the Third World – its military budgeting problems will be reduced.

But it is a risky strategy with potentially far-reaching consequences. If in Europe the allies find they are spending more and getting less, the result may be to seek a bigger say in NATO affairs. This will not be to the USA's liking. NATO jargon for a larger Western European military effort is 'strengthening the European pillar'. That is one thing, but changing the basic architecture of the alliance is another entirely. Similarly, if Western European governments also help reduce the cost of other aspects of the USA's world military role, and especially if they develop a renewed taste for global intervention, the long-term effect may be that they emerge to challenge the USA as a world power. If relative decline forces the USA to push a larger role on its allies, they may want to share not just the action and the costs but also the decision-making. Sharing the burden may end in a desire to share the power. That prospect of a new Western Europeanism grabbing a share of world power by military means is no more pleasant than if Western Europe simply continues to do the USA's bidding.

The Changing Agenda

The changing strategic context is essentially about two developments. One is the reduced confrontation between the USA and the Soviet bloc; that process can be taken further or reversed. The other is the relative decline of the USA which throws up three broad possibilities: US administrations in the 1990s may be able to shore up US leadership; Western Europe may cohere as a new power; or things may develop along the lines of the peace movements' vision.

The answer to the question posed at the outset of this chapter – who needs the peace movements? – is that we all do. But our needs will only be met if the movements themselves are sensitive and responsive to the changing context. While nuclear war is possible at any time, the immediate threat of it has diminished. The problem now is that confrontation could endure and superpower relations slide back into a new Cold War. The source of that problem is to be found only to a minor extent in the Warsaw Pact, in conservative resistance to Gorbachev's new domestic, foreign and military policies. The main source is in NATO.

NATO is capable of undermining the gains and wasting the opportunities the Gorbachev leadership has created. It is unlikely to wear him down quickly, but he would be unlikely to survive a decade of systematic rebuffs and creative delaying tactics. The stronger the peace movements are, and the more they focus on strategies to reduce confrontation, the less capable will NATO be of such negativism. This suggests three major tasks for the movements: promoting positive responses to Gorbachev's initiatives, opposing policies which sustain confrontation like new nuclear deployments and higher military spending, and generating independent initiatives for eroding it.

The movements have considerable capacity to fulfil this role. Most NATO leaders realise they must go some way towards satisfying public opinion, which is increasingly opposed to confrontation. They also know the movements are still capable of mobilising opinion. As long as this is true, they will be relatively wary about stonewalling Gorbachev and deploying new weapons systems. At a different level, continuing to communicate and meet with the independent peace groups in Eastern Europe and the USSR is also part of the strategy of eroding confrontation, for it expands the flow of ideas through what have been walls of silence.

The movements' influence extends beyond this. For years we argued with Soviet representatives about the need for unilateral initiatives – as we did with our own governments. Gorbachev's acceptance of disproportionate cuts in the INF Treaty and in CAFE shows that he has embraced the case we made to a degree. In CAFE, NATO's position focuses on a distinction between offensive and defensive force postures – which is central to the idea of defensive defence developed by researchers working on alternative concepts of security. The notion of 'reasonable sufficiency' for Soviet armed forces, which Gorbachev adopted and which underlay the initiatives in his December 1988 speech at the UN, also owes a lot to the idea of defensive defence. Neither NATO nor the Warsaw Pact has yet fully accepted the logic of defensive defence, but the limited extent to which they have is a heartening example of the strength of ideas borne by movements.

Relative US decline creates three distinct problems. The first and most immediate is the pressure from the USA for burden-sharing and 'out-of-area' operations. Both have to be resisted. Higher military spending in Western Europe will be economically and socially damaging, and in itself will help sustain confrontation. Active involvement in US adventures in the Third World will risk Europe playing a direct role in the support of oppressive regimes. The second problem is the possibility that a US administration – Bush's or a successor – will adopt the Reagan strategy of reasserting the USA's leadership of NATO through renewed Cold War. The third is the longer-term one, that Western European states may begin to think and act collectively as a new world power. This would impose political and economic costs in Western European countries themselves and in the Third World, as another competitor for power joined in the fray.

With economic integration planned by the end of 1992, Western European states are moving closer together. Many advocate developing a military component to the process. In principle, there is little reason to object to Western European states organising their security policy more closely with each other and more independently of the USA. And unless US policy and strategy changes dramatically, Western European independence from the USA is a precondition for a nuclear-free Europe.

The problem is not Western European cooperation but what sort of security it leads to. Security can mean something everybody wants, so they can be relatively free from the threat of war and enjoy a reasonable level of prosperity, democracy and justice. In the modern world, security seems unavoidably to contain an armed element, but it need not be threatening and confrontational. Western European cooperation could be aimed at common security for Europe. That would be a way of not merely eroding confrontation but ultimately ending it, creating a new framework in which different social systems exist without dangerous anatagonism. It could also be the basis for new, less exploitative relations with the Third World.

But in orthodox parlance security is also a codeword for the pursuit of power. Western European cooperation on that sort of security could be the route to its becoming the fifth world power (along with the USA, USSR, China and Japan) of the early twenty-first century, dominating and looting weaker and poorer countries. Such an approach to security necessarily rules out an end to confrontation.

The issue of what sort of security Western European cooperation pursues is actually the issue of what sort of Western Europe develops. If the peace movements do not join it the outcome may be bleak, involving both renewed confrontation with the USSR and military intervention in the Third World – whether as an independent Western European power or under US leadership. Joining that issue means movements taking their national concerns into the European context. That does not mean, for example in Britain, ignoring Trident or US bases. But it does entail accepting that the major issues are not national but international. It means addressing common European security in a global framework, not focusing on Britain or any one country with Europe and the world tacked on as afterthoughts. If the movements prove incapable of that internationalism, they cannot expect it from the rest of the population, from political parties or from governments. If they prove capable of it they will continue to be a major positive political force.

2

Bush and NATO – Comes the Reformation

ROBERT L. BOROSAGE

At the moment of its apparent triumph, the Cold War order organised by Washington is facing its most severe challenge. The decline of the Soviet Union has revealed not Washington's strength, but its weakness. The trials of the communist infidels may represent a victory for the capitalist faith, but they are also a crisis for the church. Increasingly independent allies are wearying of the costs required to sustain the institutions and rituals of the post-war order.

In no region is the growing crisis more apparent than in Western Europe, where the NATO alliance marked its fortieth anniversary in 1989. In NATO, the most devout adherents to the faith are beginning to call for a reformation. Conflicts are growing – and to address them, the people of the United States have placed a dutiful acolyte of the Cold War church at its head. The nature of George Herbert Walker Bush's administration and the constraints upon it suggest that it will have difficulty responding to the challenges it must face.

The Election – a Reaffirmation of the Faith

In an election campaign dishonest and tawdry even by US standards, Bush's statements about defence and foreign policy were limited to recitals of the Cold War catechism. Bush attacked his opponent Michael Dukakis and 'liberals' in general for being outside 'the mainstream' on defence.[1] 'The Cold War is not over', he said. The United States, while being 'bold enough to seize the opportunity for change', must also be prepared for 'protracted conflict'.[2] Calling for a 'prudent skepticism' about Gorbachev, Bush travelled to Fulton, Missouri, to invoke the authority of Winston Churchill for a continued policy of 'peace through strength'. He denied that Mikhail Gorbachev represented any kind of fundamental change or 'turning inward', and told the West to keep its defences up:

Where we have seen flexibility, it has come because the price of aggression is too high – because we supported the Mujahadeen in Afghanistan. It has come because intimidation failed – because we deployed the Pershing and Cruise missiles in Europe ... The evidence is clear ... the Soviets ... are restrained by our strength, our ability to deter aggression, the unity of the democracies.[3]

In his position papers and speeches, Bush never deviated from the gospel. He questioned Dukakis's commitment to modernising strategic and short-range nuclear weapons, both of which are said to be vital to deterrence in Europe. He dismissed calls to cut back US forces in Europe: 'Under present circumstances no changes in the present level of our commitment are anticipated ... I can assure our allies that America has no intention of "decoupling" or weakening our commitment to European defense. NATO is the best investment in peace we have ever made.'[4]

Bush embraced the growing bipartisan belief that Reagan's policy of 'peace through strength' had produced Gorbachev's concessions on INF missiles, Afghanistan, Angola. For believers, peace through strength requires not only a continued build-up of military forces, but also a willingness to use them in pursuit of US interests.[5] Pre-emptive diplomacy as in the Philippines against Ferdinand Marcos, punitive raids in Libya against Colonel Qaddafi, Low-Intensity Conflict as exemplified by intervention in El Salvador – these provide verse for a fateful renewal of the interventionist cast US policy has taken.

At the same time, faced with large budget deficits and wedded to a pledge not to raise taxes, Bush's campaign acknowledged that while military build-up must continue, the military budget would not rise significantly if at all. The trivial nature of the campaign enabled Bush to keep his priorities among the mysteries. The budget would be balanced with no new taxes – a 'flexible freeze' on spending would be the elixir. All major military weapons systems would be developed but the military budget would not increase – the magic potion would be better management and 'competitive strategies'. The rhetoric invoked the gospel; the programme demanded a leap of faith.

The Bush Team – Reassertion of the Churchmen

That Bush was elected to preserve the conservative flame but turn down the heat was reflected in his initial security appointments. Absent were the burning zealots of reaction, the Jeanne Kirkpatricks, Caspar Weinbergers and Bill Caseys. Instead, the administration was to be dominated by dutiful attendants of the church.

The most powerful, Secretary of State James Baker (Bush's friend and confidant of 40 years) gained a reputation as a 'pragmatist' in the Reagan years. A skilled and cynical political operator (he master-minded Bush's low road campaign) Baker is noted neither for great vision nor imagination. Instead he is seen as a practical, extraordinarily able manager of conventional conservative beliefs. For example, as Reagan's Secretary of the Treasury, Baker was responsible for the 'Baker plan' for managing the Third World debt crisis. The plan called for bilateral negotiations in which debtor countries would pledge internal economic austerity in exchange for further loans. The plan succeeded in preventing any major default, in continuing the flow of payments to money-centre banks in the North, in reinforcing the competitive decline in commodity prices. It also further impoverished the Third World, contributed to a stagnation in global trade, and injured US exporters while aiding US financial institutions and multinationals. It was an operational success and a conceptual and human disaster.

Bush's National Security Advisor, the retired general Brent Scowcroft, served in a similar post under Gerald Ford. He is a cautious, unimaginative strategist who has yet to be caught committing an original thought in public. John Tower, the first nominee for Defense Secretary, might have carried the conservative torch; his defeat was a graphic display of the weaknesses of the Bush mandate. Representative Richard Cheney is a sober, conservative manager respected for the solidity of his views, not for the originality of his imagination.

The Bush team is able, conservative, politically sophisticated. It will seek to defend the given order in an evolving world, working to defuse and limit heresy and challenge. As one congressional source concluded: 'The Bush team is made up of pragmatic but deeply traditional people. It's an outlook that's still in the confrontational mode, as if deterring Soviet expansionist aggression is still the dominant problem ... The hand of the past will be on the tiller.'[6]

Trials – the Global Constraints

This conservative team comes into office in a situation very different from that facing Ronald Reagan eight years ago. Reagan's election in 1980 was foreshadowed by broad national support for a renewed crusade against the Soviet Union and communism. The financial elite was concerned by the wave of Third World revolutions, which culminated in 1979 with the Sandinistas' victory in Nicaragua. Then there was the fall of the Shah in Iran, the victory of the New Jewel Movement in Grenada, the Soviet Union's invasion of Afghanistan. The security mandarins were waging a fierce inquisition against the mild heresies of the Carter years. Led by groups like the Committee on the Present Danger, they raised national alarm about 'Soviet nuclear superiority', the 'window of vulnerability', the Soviet 'threat to Europe'. The

US public, traumatised by the energy crisis, stagflation and US citizens held hostage in Iran, expressed overwhelming support for more military spending. Reagan had a clear mandate. And he immediately launched the largest military build-up in peacetime history.

In 1989, both the national mood and the strategic perspective are very different. Gorbachev's initiatives and concessions have dulled the spectre of the Soviet infidel. The economic and financial elite, now focused on US budget and trade deficits, is willing to accept limits on military spending to gain cutbacks in social programmes. At the polls, the public is overwhelmingly against further increases in military spending. Even the high priests of the strategic brotherhood recognise, in Kissinger's words, that 'the postwar era in international relations is coming to an end'.[7]

Kissinger joined Cyrus Vance, Carter's former Secretary of State, to summarise the centrist view in *Foreign Affairs*, the foreign policy organ of the East coast establishment. The view they expressed was as follows: the USA's nuclear monopoly has ended; the USA's relative share of the world economy is less than half what it was 40 years ago. The Soviet threat seems to have diminished; other countries – Japan, Western Europe, the newly industrialised countries, 'already have had a major impact on U.S. interests'. 'New issues' such as 'state-sponsored terrorism and international drug trafficking have become urgent'.

The first priority must be to secure the USA's place in the new world economy. Almost plaintively, the two mandarins note that 'the weakness of the U.S. economy may be among the most serious and urgent foreign policy challenges to the next president ... It is increasingly obvious that our military prowess and even our nuclear capabilities do not by themselves contribute to the struggle for international markets.'[8]

Gone is the triumphal aura of the church militant that framed the Reagan era. Pessimism and confusion are spreading among the initiates. The editors of *Foreign Affairs* opened their issue on the year 1989 with a picture of the United States 'in a strange position', 'beset' by large budget deficits and huge trade imbalances and 'threatened' by intractable Third World debt. America's hegemonic economic strength is under question.[9]

The perceived need for an American revival has prompted direct concern about competition with the USA's allies. A growing list of economic disputes with Western Europe greeted the incoming administration – access to the European market, West German economic expansion to help cut the US trade deficits, support for the dollar, limits on trade and credits with the East bloc. *Foreign Affairs*'s editorial warns: 'For decades we have encouraged the European dream of unity, but now the reality may become more of a nightmare for us.'[10]

The most difficult questions relating to Western Europe concern the cost of NATO, the central pillar of the Cold War church. For decades, US military planning, force structure and missions, weapons development and spending have been justified largely by the commitment to defend the allies from a threatened Soviet attack. Yet now, Europe is stable. The allies are prosperous. The enemy is in internal disarray – it is neither seductive nor threatening. Social and political disorders in the Third World are attracting more of the security priesthood's attention; they offer more scope for action. Constraints on the available resources demand a clear set of priorities. But to alter the priority given to NATO would be to call into question the basic tenets of the faith.

The muddled perspective that such a view of affairs produces was illustrated in *Discriminate Deterrence*, the controversial attempt by conservative strategists to give a coherent statement of the USA's long-range military strategy. With a charter from President and Congress, the Commission on Integrated Long-Range Strategy enlisted the most trusted of the initiates – Kissinger, Zbigniew Brzezinski, Samuel P. Huntington, Fred Iklé and Albert Wohlstetter – to shape defence policies for the 1990s. Their report charts new powers on the rise and the relative decline of the Soviet Union. It acknowledges the increasing importance of economic competition to the USA and the increasing limits on US military spending. It suggests that for too long, disproportionate resources have been spent on defence against the most improbable threat – a Soviet invasion of Western Europe:

> An emphasis on massive Soviet attacks leads to tunnel vision among defense planners ... An excessive focus on these contingencies diverts defense planners from trying to deal with many important and far more plausible situations.[11]

While it describes the US commitment to Western Europe as unshakeable, *Discriminate Deterrence* recommends that the US devote more attention and resources to limited conflicts on the European periphery and in the Third World generally. It acknowledges that budgetary limitations require choices in strategy and weaponry.

Yet having laid the ground for major revision of the doctrine, the commissioners seem to get scared by their own hints of heresy. Their final recommendations are an embrace of orthodoxy, calling for more of almost everything – new strategic nuclear weapons, new short-range nuclear weapons, investment in strategic defence, more investment in high-tech conventional weapons, more military aid, covert operations and rapid deployment forces, more emphasis on Low Intensity

Conflict. The need for change and choice is apparent, but change seems to call the very faith into question. The Bush administration entered power with the most devout Cold War theologians unable to point the way to reform.

Tribulations – NATO Doctrine and European Heresy

Nowhere is the need for a revision of the doctrine more apparent than in NATO. The heart of NATO's strategy is 'extended deterrence' – the USA's promise to start a nuclear war if the USSR were to attack the West. From the moment the Soviet Union became able to eradicate the USA with nuclear weapons, NATO defence strategy was rendered implausible, if not impossible. Kissinger put it best (once he was out of office):

> Mutual suicide cannot be made to appear as a rational option ... Our European allies should not keep asking us to multiply strategic assurances that we cannot possibly mean, or if we do mean, we should not want to execute because if we executed them we risk the destruction of civilization ... [12]

To make the promise of salvation through suicide more credible, US nuclear theologists developed the doctrine of 'flexible response' (of which *Discriminate Deterrence* is an updated version). It calls for the use of conventional forces, then tactical and short-range nuclear weapons, then European-based weapons to deter the Soviets. The strategic claim is that such capacity bolsters deterrence and makes war less likely. The unstated but inescapable hope is that if war were to start, it might be limited to Europe.

For obvious reasons, *Discriminate Deterrence* is not too appealing to European leaders, who want to ensure that if the USA starts a nuclear war, it puts itself at risk too. People in Western Europe are displaying less and less enthusiasm for leaving their fate up to the United States. Long before Reagan's errancies, Washington's claim to papal infallibility raised serious doubts even among the faithful.

Beneath the disagreements lies the true crisis of faith, which hinges on the very different assessments of the threat posed by the Soviet Union. US strategists and NATO doctrine assume that the threat is constant and deterrence fragile. Meanwhile more and more Europeans are thinking the threat more fanciful than not and deterrence more than adequate. To limit 'early reliance' on nuclear weapons, military planners want to boost conventional forces. But there is scant political support for increased conventional spending against an increasingly improbable threat.

The Reagan administration exacerbated these differences. Washington maintained that its commitment to Europe was unshakeable, but conservative strategists placed increasing emphasis on the greater urgency of other obligations. Reagan's administration regularly called for shared responsibility, but acted unilaterally. The Pentagon asserted the need to bolster nuclear deterrence in Europe, yet Reagan seemed cavalier about trading this away in Reykjavik in 1986. Washington wanted new conventional and nuclear weapons to strengthen flexible response, but Reagan's promise to render nuclear weapons 'impotent and obsolete' through the Strategic Defense Initiative seemed at the very least to question the nature of the USA's guarantee to Western Europe.

The INF Treaty has further highlighted the differences. The removal of land-based intermediate nuclear weapons from Europe alarmed NATO strategists, most of whom had looked on the 'zero option' as a political ploy designed only to place the USSR on the defensive and ensure deployment of Cruise and Pershing 2 missiles went ahead (see Chapter 1). The Treaty did not usher in a new era for the doctrinists. As far as they were concerned, the 'Soviet threat' remained – perhaps it was made more dangerous by the allies' growing 'allergy' to nuclear weapons. Deterrence was still fragile; will had to be demonstrated. Military doctrine demanded that NATO's defences be bolstered. NATO planning councils ratified the imperative of modernising short-range nuclear weapons, new deployments of air- and sea-based Cruise missiles, and developing high-tech, deep-strike conventional technologies to strengthen deterrence.[13]

But modernisation would be costly. With Washington already facing cutbacks in military spending, US strategists called upon the Western Europeans to bear more of the burden. Brzezinski summarised the consensus view:

> Since Europe can and should do more for its defense, and since the United States has to make more of a defense effort elsewhere but cannot afford to do so, it follows that a gradual but significant re-adjustment in burden-sharing is necessary and will occur.[14]

The response to the INF Treaty in Western European political circles was varied, but it diverged from scripture. Even the conservative government in West Germany had little appetite for a new fight on nuclear modernisation (see Chapter 4). Despite ritual pledges in NATO planning councils, British and West German military budgets were going down, not up.

The accord was widely viewed as a prelude to a new era. The late

Franz-Josef Strauss, arch-reactionary head of the West German Christian Socialist Union (CSU), returned from Moscow and declared that the post-war period was over and that the West need no longer fear that the USSR had 'offensive, aggressive intentions'.[15] Gorbachev's call for a 'common European home' struck a deep chord. When West Europeans looked East, they saw not infidels in search of a new crusade, but peoples sharing a common heritage, undergoing political and economic difficulties but open to teaching and conversion, to commerce and exchange. The allies remained loyal to the church – there was little talk of leaving NATO. But a reformation of the doctrine seemed increasingly desirable. And very few could imagine increasing their contributions to a military force that seemed part of the past.

The resulting dilemma facing the Bush administration is reflected in a memorandum drafted by Bush's excessively praised National Security Advisor Scowcroft and analyst R. James Woolsey for *American Agenda*, a bipartisan report prepared by former Presidents Gerald Ford and Jimmy Carter. On defence spending, Scowcroft and Woolsey write that the alliance must 'compensate' for the reduction in US nuclear forces under the INF Treaty. But the nature of the necessary modernisation is not clear. 'More reliance on strategic nuclear forces' would be helpful, but with the reductions sought under the Strategic Arms Reductions Talks such reliance is unlikely to be 'reassuring' to the allies. Modernisation of short-range theatre nuclear weapons 'is important', but faces great 'political resistance'. Some conventional force improvements are 'quite important' but face 'cost constraints'. New long-range munitions (for example, scatterable mines and precision-guided munitions) offer promise, but 'sensible steps ... have proven to be politically difficult in Europe'.

For Woolsey and Scowcroft, burden-sharing is a 'potentially explosive issue', but perhaps a substantially heavier commitment to 'national specialization' would be possible. Europe could take on an increased share of the manpower requirements for NATO ground forces while the USA concentrated more on tactical aircraft and other support units.[16] This would also mean Europe was financially assisting US military manufacture. Neither Scowcroft nor Woolsey express confidence that the allies will accept this burden.

For Bush, who accepted the presidential nomination by listing the 'missions assigned, missions accomplished', the mission is far from clear. New constraints on and challenges to Washington require change and cutbacks, particularly in Western Europe. Cold War doctrine demands constancy and re-commitment, particularly in Western Europe. In the face of growing heresy and calls for reformation, a reaffirmation of the faith seems vital. Resolving these conflicting currents will not be an easy job.

More Tribulations – the Domestic Political Context

When Reagan was elected in 1980, the popular culture heralded his victory by turning a turgid pop-economic tract, George Gilder's *Wealth and Power*, into a national best-seller. Bush's election was preceded by a similar cultural phenomenon – only this time *The Rise and Fall of the Great Powers* by obscure Yale professor Paul Kennedy was a warning against 'imperial overstretch'. When Reagan was elected he led a conservative onslaught, defeating the incumbent with a campaign based on conservative ideas. Hard-knuckle right-wing campaigns beat leading liberal senators and gave the Republicans control of the Senate for the first time in over 20 years. Chastened Democrats scrambled to endorse the President's supply-side economic policy and Cold War agenda.

In 1988, Bush won the presidency with a disingenuous campaign that provided no mandate other than the oft-repeated and widely disbe-lieved pledge not to raise taxes. For the first time in history, the party of the victorious presidential candidate lost seats in the Senate and the House of Representatives at the federal level; and suffered reverses in statehouses and legislatures at the local level. Bush faces a feisty Congress, eager to hold him to his 'kinder, gentler nation' promises.

Reagan began his presidency with a clear domestic agenda: to cut taxes, slash domestic spending, deregulate corporations and build up the military. He focused on domestic issues, putting major foreign policy initiatives on the back burner. When Secretary of State Al Haig would not cooperate, he was summarily dispatched.

Bush begins his presidency facing a domestic stalemate. The budget deficit, the crisis in the savings and loans banks, a major corruption scandal which surfaced in mid-1988, and the need for corporate re-regulation presage domestic political squabbles with no clear resolu-tion in sight. So Bush is very likely to think an active approach to foreign policy essential to gaining political stature and support at home. His selection of James Baker places the strongest member of the cabinet at the head of the State Department.

The Bush team faces immediate domestic pressures as far as the NATO alliance is concerned. The budget fight, which will consume attention in the first Bush term, is likely to raise demands for cutbacks in spending on NATO and for 'burden-sharing' to enable the USA to reduce its troop commitments and cut its budget.

Even before Bush was elected, heretical thoughts about the costs of NATO had been tinting the political spectrum. On the right, neo-conservatives led by Irving Kristol dismissed the 'nuclear umbrella' – the USA's strategic 'guarantee' to Western Europe – as a sham, and derided the Europeans for being infected with 'social democracy' and unwilling to bear their fair share of the burdens of defence. Kristol and others argued that the United States should leave the alliance and free itself to act unilaterally in its own interests.[17] On the left, progressives led by Jesse Jackson and Representative Patricia Schroeder called for the allies to bear a greater share of the burden so that the USA could reduce military forces and spending.[18] Even high priests like Kissinger and Brzezinski called for Europe to take greater responsibility for conventional defence, so that the United States could focus on evolving threats in the Persian Gulf and elsewhere.[19]

The Fiscal Crisis of the Cold War Church

After increasing the budget by 40 per cent in real terms in his first five years, Reagan found his projected build-up stalled by the budget crisis. Over Reagan's last three years military spending actually declined in real terms.[20]

Bush has shown himself even less able to sustain military spending. He has little of Reagan's political prowess and faces a raucous clamour from Wall Street, Main Street and foreign investors to bring down budget deficits. The USA's budget deficit is still running at about $150 billion a year. Major new expenditures are needed – $50 billion to refurbish nuclear weapons production plants, $50–100 billion to bail out federally guaranteed savings and loans banks, $10–15 billion in promises made by Bush for a 'kinder, gentler' agenda. Long-delayed investments in social and physical infrastructure must be made. Bush has pledged not to cut social security expenditures and not to raise taxes. The Reagan years exhausted most of the politically acceptable cuts in domestic spending. That makes the military the focus of attention.

Pentagon planning under Reagan's Defense Secretary Frank Carlucci called for 2 per cent real growth over the Fiscal Years 1990–4. Even this has meant cuts of $250 billion in previously projected spending for the period. Yet approval for even 2 per cent real growth will be difficult to gain. Conservative Democrat Senator Sam Nunn, the influential Chair of the Senate Armed Services Committee, believes that military spending will be lucky to achieve 'no-growth' over the period. National Security Advisor Scowcroft acknowledged that even steady military budgets would require 'a fight'. Bush's budget plans increase military spending for Fiscal Year 1990 only by what is necessary to match inflation, followed by 1 per cent increases over inflation in the following two years, and a 2 per cent real increase for 1993. Zero growth budgets would force additional cuts of another $140 billion from the five-year plan.

In the coming budget fight, NATO will surely attract significant attention, if only for the same reason that bank robber Willy Sutton had: 'because that is where the money is'. In 1985, the Pentagon estimated that NATO consumed 58 per cent of its budget – some $160 billion. With one-third of the US Army's standing divisions in Europe and another whose primary mission is European defence, NATO reductions offer significant annual savings. Analysts estimate that withdrawing and dismantling one-half of the US forces assigned to NATO could save about $67 billion a year.[21] If money is not saved in Europe, it must be cut from major weapons systems or force reductions. Already Representative Les Aspin, Chair of the House Armed Services Committee, has suggested that the B-2 Stealth Bomber, the Midgetman missile, the Seawolf submarine and two new aircraft carrier task forces may have to be eliminated or cut. The inevitable inter-service battles will add military support – particularly from the Navy and Air Force – for troop reductions in Western Europe, together with demands that US allies share more of the burden.[22]

Yet no rational person truly believes that increased military spending will be easily forthcoming from the allies. The result is that the prudent churchmen counsel delay, compromise, coordination. The memorandum written for the Carter–Ford report by Lawrence Eagleburger (nominated to be James Baker's deputy at State) and Warren Christopher (who held a similar position under Cyrus Vance) displayed the advice that Bush will get. Eagleburger and Christopher write that the response to the budget crisis is 'fundamental to effective US foreign policy. American credibility abroad will stand or fall on whether the President and Congress can make difficult decisions at home.'

They accept that military budgets will not rise. Choices must be made. But, they warn, the US should not keep trying to pressurise the allies to increase military spending. After 1992, when Western Europe should be more unified and a new US administration will be in place, the US should hope for a 'more effective integration of the defense establishment'. The Europeans will return to the fold, but the USA must not pressure them:

Indeed we should urge that over time a larger share of the burden be shifted to Western Europe. But to push too hard and too fast for substantial increased spending on defense, especially when the US is cutting back, would cut across what we believe you should try to do which is to persuade the Western Europeans that we are entering a new time in which the need for cooperative action will be essential.

The emphasis of the new Administration should be on that word 'cooperative'.[23]

A Stranger Bearing Gifts

In December 1988, while Bush was still appointing his cabinet and making his initial plans, Mikhail Gorbachev came to New York to offer his 'Christmas present' in an historic speech at the United Nations. Cold War theologians quickly dismissed Gorbachev's vision of a world beyond conflict, dubbing his reference to the common challenges facing all people utopian rhetoric. But his pledge to reduce Soviet forces unilaterally by 500,000 troops, including disbanding six tank and artillery divisions and removing 50,000 troops, 5,000 tanks, artillery and river-crossing materials from East Germany, Czechoslovakia and Hungary stunned even military planners. President Reagan declared that he had every reason to 'trust' the Soviet leader. Secretary of State George Shultz described the reductions as a 'welcome and significant step in the right direction'.[24]

Gorbachev's initiative and vision won him public approval in the USA. Representative Schroeder called the proposal 'just the opportunity we need to get our deficit under control'. Senator James Sasser, Chair of the Senate Budget Committee, predicted that it would be difficult to hold military spending steady and 'almost impossible' to raise it.

The anointed rushed to defend the faith. Nothing had changed; the sins were unredeemed. The Soviets would still have conventional superiority in Europe; Gorbachev's seductions must be resisted. The NATO ministers congratulated him for the initiative, but called for far deeper cuts as part of negotiated reductions. At the same time, however, West German Foreign Minister Hans Dietrich Genscher called for the postponement once again of any decision to modernise short-range nuclear missiles. Writing on the editorial page of the *Washington Post*, Kissinger fulminated against the 'West's wishful thinkers'. 'The question is not whether [Gorbachev] is serious, but whether the West is', he said. He dismissed Gorbachev's initiative: 'the general perception that Gorbachev has put forward unilateral concessions is nonsense, or true only in a highly formal sense'.

For Kissinger, Gorbachev was brilliantly serving his own interests. His statements would increase 'obstacles' to modernising short-range nuclear weapons, conventional weapons and burden-sharing. 'NATO could easily wind up with no military strategy at all.' Gorbachev had put NATO to the test. Kissinger called for the Bush administration not to let itself be 'stampeded', to define its own agenda and timetable for a 'serious dialogue', not 'public relations spectacles'.[25]

Senator Nunn offered a similar view from the faithful opposition. For Nunn, Gorbachev's move presented the alliance with 'significant challenges'. According to the Senator, the only response is to proceed with business as usual. Make Soviet unilateral reductions part of a negotiating process so they can be verified. Demand on-site inspection for these unilateral cuts. Continue with increased specialisation in the 'roles and missions' of each country in NATO. Begin a 'sustained program of vigorous public education' to gain public support for military.[26]

But such ritual reassurance could not mask the reality now facing the alliance. Its commitment of enormous cost is premised on a threat the plausibility of which is diminishing. The imminent threat posed by the Soviet infidel which provided the justification for all this expense, bother and risk seems part of another age. When even the staunch Margaret Thatcher greeted the President-elect by announcing that the 'Cold War is over', and 'major decisions face the West', the tidings of the reformation were clear.

The Keepers of the Church

Bush and his appointees said little in Gorbachev's wake. Asked about his response, Reagan said the US would cut its own forces 'only if we were left with supriority'. Bush said only, 'I support what the President says.' Reagan beamed and patted Bush on the arm.[27]

The primary policy reaction by the Bush team was to buy time. He announced that his administration would have to delay the scheduled February reopening of the Strategic Arms Reduction Talks in order to undertake a general review of US strategic planning. He announced that he had told Gorbachev there would be no quick response, that his team 'would need time' to give the proposals 'a hard Bush administration look'.[28] Later, Bush aides reported that a 'sweeping review' of US strategic goals and strategies would be 'a lengthy process'.[29]

Once the temporising ends, the administration's response will most likely be sculpted and managed by Secretary of State Baker. As a former Treasury Secretary, Baker is intimately involved with the economic challenges facing the United States. When he was Chief of Staff in the White House, he was a wily bureaucratic operator who maintained excellent relations with the press and Congress. And as Bush's long-time friend, he is personally close to the President who relies upon his judgement. Baker has little foreign policy experience outside the critical economic negotiations which he managed as Treasury Secretary. But this may be the perfect background for a Secretary of State at a time when securing the USA's economic position is widely viewed as the first security policy.

Since his appointment, Baker has been virtually invisible. Earlier, he offered a brief insight into his priorities to the *Wall Street Journal*, fittingly the paper of record for US financial circles: 'The scope of the national security debate has been broadened to include the economic dimension', Baker said, 'and I think the reason is that the economic domination of the United States, which has long been taken for granted, is to some extent now being questioned.' Baker suggested that the alliance be viewed in this context:

> Burden-sharing is more than the number of troops and planes. We need to consider the economic factor. For too long in the US, we have thought of it as strictly a national-security issue, with no economic component. But those days are gone. You can't argue with that guy in Congress whose urban grant you're trying to phase out to support pre-positioning of more US troops in South Korea, when the Koreans are running up a big trade surplus with us.[30]

For Baker, Western Europe and Japan will be the major focus of attention. His mission will be to gain consensus on common strategy versus the Soviet Union, while winning concessions on economic issues of concern to Washington, like access to Western European markets after 1992, West German and Japanese reflation to aid US exports, coordination on Third World debt and trade and credits to the East.

Baker is a consummate politician, not an ideologue. He will counsel compromise in one arena to gain agreement in another. If his record as Treasury Secretary and Chief of Staff is any guide, he will seek coordination and cooperation through increased communication. At the same time, he will separate questions and seek bilateral agreements to short-circuit multilateral discussions. So if Baker's history is the best clue to Bush's strategy, we can expect a furious round of negotiations with ally and adversary alike. Negotiations need not end in agreements to be successful. Baker can use international negotiations to fend off congressional demands for unilateral military cuts. He can use congressional pressures at home to seek concessions from allies abroad.

At the same time, the Bush administration will seek to use sophisticated public spectacles and news management to gain popular support at home and among the allies. At home, early leaks suggested the administration will put forward low-cost 'kinder, gentler' initiatives (a literacy review corps to teach adult illiterates, housing reforms to encourage private ownership of public houses, a children's agenda on day care and pre-natal care for women) to gain political support before entering the budget fight. Abroad, consultation, strategic review and fact-finding missions will provide the appearance of reform and initiative. Respected mandarins will be enlisted to restate the gospel. The goal will be as far as possible to preserve the *status quo*, not to revise it.

The Bush team is also likely to seek an opportunity to use military force to demonstrate its toughness. The campaign at the end of 1988 about the Rabta chemical plant in Libya, where it was alleged chemical weapons were being made, seemed a possible prelude to a quick bombing raid. Other opportunities may present themselves as time goes by, against Libya or some other target in the Middle East. Such action would be popular at home, and warn ally and adversary alike that the USA is prepared to use military force in defence of its interests.

With tactical flexibility and political sophistication, Bush and Baker will seek to reunite the church and muffle the calls for reformation. The economic and budgetary constraints on the United States may dictate change, but the institutions and theologians of the national security church will resist this mightily. It is difficult to imagine Bush and Baker attempting anything more ambitious than a willingness to update the scripture to sustain loyalty to the church. If the reformation does come, it will be against the wiles and wishes of Washington.

3

'New Thinking' and Soviet Strategy

GERARD HOLDEN

The 'Soviet threat' has been one of the most useful political tools in sustaining post-war transatlantic capitalism. By the same token, it has opened up wide divisions within peace movements and parties which tried in any way to challenge the structures of Atlanticism. Writers like Alan Wolfe have documented some of the processes of creating the threat perception.[1] But to focus exclusively on the excesses of Western alarmism risks ignoring the real questions that need to be answered about Soviet policy.

Mikhail Gorbachev's reforms and projected reforms of Soviet security policy and military strategy have created problems for various analyses of the USSR from right, left and centre. The right's traditional view has always been that the USSR wanted either territory or political leverage in Western Europe. The first variant has always been unconvincing despite its simplicity, and few people seriously believed it. But the less crude argument about political leverage has always been more difficult to pin down, and thus to challenge. On the left – or parts of it – changes in Soviet policy and strategy have been a non-issue: the Soviet threat never existed, so why discuss the evolution of Soviet policy? A more centrist argument has held that while there may once have been a genuine confrontation in central Europe and a threat of Soviet aggression, this danger has decreased steadily over time,[2] and Europe can no longer be the cause of a war between East and West.

The problem for the centrist argument is that although it is indeed now difficult to see Europe as a *casus belli*, the rest of the analysis is historically dubious. It misses a large and valid part of the left's argument about the roots of the Cold War, which questions the reality of the Soviet threat in the immediate post-war period. It also tends to underestimate the difficulties of negotiating reduced military confrontation in Europe, and the complex interconnections between politics, military technologies and strategies in the region. In fact, both sides have taken more offensive postures even during periods of political detente, according to the 'logic' of military requirements.

Gorbachev's disarmament diplomacy has unsettled the right. Its evident purpose of undermining the image of the 'Soviet threat' has had considerable success. At the same time – inconveniently for the more narrow-minded sections of the left – Gorbachev and other Soviet commentators have virtually admitted that elements in the USSR's military posture might have seemed to pose a threat in the past, even though none was intended. Such admissions introduced an important new element into the debate about European security, by conceding a central point made by Western European alternative defence analysts: that changes in the Soviet posture are necessary in the long term for any alternative European security system.

As well as the Soviet military stance towards Europe, another central component of the European security system is of course the political role played by Soviet forces within the Warsaw Treaty Organisation (WTO). Given their evidently repressive actions in a succession of Eastern European post-war crises, it has been hard to see how European security as a whole could be reshaped without some change in the Soviet–East European relationship. Soviet interventions in Eastern Europe have not only served to repress aspirations to more national autonomy and democratic socialism in the East. By seeming to legitimise US hegemony within NATO, they have also given a seemingly strong argument to Western supporters of the *status quo.*

Gorbachev's leadership has not removed these problems. It is still less than ten years since martial law was imposed in Poland. A reforming leadership in the USSR has in the past (particularly under Khrushchev) been a destabilising and partly unwelcome influence for some Eastern European leaderships. But there does seem to be a different approach under Gorbachev. He seems to realise that any future military intervention in Eastern Europe would be disastrous for both domestic and foreign policy reforms, and he seems to be beginning to re-examine past interventions.

Against this background, the late 1980s have been a particularly important time for observers of Soviet security policy and its impact on the West. In this chapter I shall try to pick out the most significant recent developments and make some assessment of their prospects in the 1990s.

Strategic Shifts

Under Gorbachev, shifts in military strategy have been instituted or projected in both nuclear and conventional fields. The term 'reasonable sufficiency' (*razumnaya dostatochnost*) which Gorbachev introduced in 1986 was presented as having both nuclear and conventional applications. It was a new criterion for the level of forces needed to ensure Soviet security while allowing disarmament to take place. 'Reasonable sufficiency' is also an aspect of the more general reassessment of foreign policy which has been labelled 'new thinking'. 'New thinking' incorporates a number of features: a recognition of the interdependence of national and international security; a view of security as a political rather than a military-technical problem in the nuclear age; a recognition of the need for flexibility and compromise in negotiations; and a more comprehensive understanding of international security, covering the military, economic, political, humanitarian and ecological spheres.

A number of these approaches are similar to Western ideas of 'common security'. Their more directly military aspects tie in with Soviet writings of the 1970s and early 1980s, which challenged the traditional view that the arms race was simply imposed on an unwilling USSR, and its continuation had little to do with Soviet actions.[3] But Stephen Shenfield has also identified elements of rethinking which owe more to a Marxist – or at least Soviet – view of international relations in the nuclear era. Shenfield's argument is that the risk of nuclear war confronted Soviet thinking with a dilemma because it threw into doubt the inevitability of a communist future for humanity. The ensuing debate proposed international interdependence rather than growing socialist strength as the crucial factor helping detente, and put 'peace' over 'socialism' as the goal of Soviet foreign policy. As a result more restraint in foreign policy was needed and non-military factors became more important in the global 'correlation of forces'.[4]

The practical implications of this reassessment became apparent in Gorbachev's disarmament diplomacy from late 1985 onwards. As far as nuclear forces were concerned, 'reasonable sufficiency' seemed to amount to something close to minimum deterrence. Gorbachev's three-stage plan for nuclear disarmament by the year 2000 was not presented as leading to a levelling-off at minimum deterrence levels, but detailed public backup papers produced by Soviet scholars seemed to view minimum deterrence as a more feasible goal than total denuclearisation. Even so, the new flexibility of Soviet diplomacy contributed much to the conclusion of the Intermediate Nuclear Forces (INF) Treaty in late 1987, in the course of which the USSR accepted asymmetrical cuts and, in effect, a measure of unilateral disarmament.

The nuclear implications of 'reasonable sufficiency' can be summarised as greater flexibility and an abandonment of strictly numerical measures of 'parity'. The consequences for conventional forces were less immediately apparent, but potentially just as far-reaching. The term was first applied in the context of Soviet/WTO forces in Europe. Their apparently offensive configuration had long been cited by the right as evidence of the 'Soviet threat', and it caused concern to alternative defence proponents. However, even before the signs of a Soviet reassessment of conventional postures emerged, there was a case against orthodox conceptions of the 'Soviet threat'. Michael MccGwire of the Brookings Institution has reconstructed Soviet decision-making not as a desire for territorial expansion or political pressure on Western Europe. Instead he suggests a conventional offensive was seen as a last resort to try to prevent the nuclear devastation of the USSR *if and only if* war with the West already seemed inevitable.[5] The distinction is crucial: most Western writing on Soviet military policy has traditionally been too self-restricting to appreciate its significance. Nor has the WTO ever had the kind of superiority to give it a serious chance of succeeding in carrying out the strategy successfully, though this is a slightly different issue.

Gorbachev began to address the 'Soviet threat' problem in early 1986 in his speech to the 27th CPSU Congress. Here he seemed to acknowledge the existence of Western fears, however misguided, and implicitly criticised Soviet military planning:

> The Soviet military doctrine is entirely in keeping with the letter and spirit of the initiatives we have put forward. Its orientation is unequivocally defensive. In the military sphere we intend to act in such a way as to give nobody grounds for fears, even imagined, about their security.[6]

There then followed a number of statements from Soviet figures and bodies of the WTO, stressing the need for defensive military doctrines on both sides and proposing that discussion of these should be included on the East–West negotiating agenda. The WTO and USSR also adjusted their definitions of 'military doctrine' to make war-prevention its main focus – as against planning for the conduct of war.

Initial Western responses were sceptical, but two factors did seem to be at work which suggested practical changes might follow or indeed be already under way, to a limited extent. First, Gorbachev seemed to be aware of the political *dis*utility of an offensive military posture that seemed to threaten Western Europe, with which the USSR was seeking improved relations. Second, as Soviet literature became more explicit about Soviet strategy, it became harder for anyone in the West to argue that the new approach was just a tactic to put NATO in the dock over its own doctrines, for example of nuclear first use. In mid-1988 academic commentator Alexei Arbatov explicitly analysed the discrepancies between declared and actual military policy: 'While the military doctrine maintained its purely defensive nature, strategy, tactics and, accordingly, individual areas of the military buildup had an increasingly offensive orientation'.[7]

As a way of assessing these developments, it may be useful to outline two contrasting explanations offered by Western observers during the course of 1988. In an extension of his earlier treatment of Soviet strategy, MccGwire argued that the changes could be traced to a reassessment made in the early 1980s. He argued that at that time the Soviet leadership saw a significantly higher risk of conflict with the USA in the Persian Gulf, but considered such a conflict would not necessarily escalate to world war. In those circumstances, according to MccGwire, it was decided that the offensive in Western Europe which had previously been considered essential was no longer so; hence it was possible to adopt a more defensive posture there.

A rather different explanation was offered by Jack Snyder. He argued that the conventional offensive option had not been a rationally calculated strategy (as MccGwire assumed) but the result of domestic political and bureaucratic battles – parts of the Soviet military establishment sought to protect their own interests by insisting on the importance of the offensive. Gorbachev wanted to challenge these entrenched institutions, which were likely to resist. Both Snyder and MccGwire considered it likely that the detailed working-out of the new policy at the military-technical level would be a long process, possibly involving disagreements between political and military institutions, but MccGwire considered these disagreements less critical.[8]

Internal and External Processes

I have already suggested a considerable range of influences which may have been at work behind the public pronouncements about Soviet strategy. Domestic ideological rethinking, hard-headed strategic reassessments, a new ability to see the USSR from the outside, and the influence of Western ideas of common security and alternative defence are all possibilities which I have outlined or hinted at. But it is worth examining this combination of factors in more detail, as their relative importance will be significant in the 1990s.

The problem can be seen in microcosm in the dispute over who should take credit for the INF Treaty. At stake in the INF row was whether credit should go to Gorbachev for Soviet flexibility, to Western peace movements for challenging their own governments and leading the USSR on to new ideas, or to NATO for ultimately achieving an advantageous agreement after insisting on negotiation from strength. The straightforward NATO line was a weak argument, because the Treaty undeniably undermined NATO's strategy of 'flexible response' as it was officially supposed to exist. This led to uncertainties over 'compensation' for Cruise and Pershing 2. But the peace movement's claim that the agreement had nothing to do with Western strength and Soviet negotiation from weakness is not fully convincing either. Even without going into the Soviet motives behind the specific concessions made in 1986–7, it is hard to avoid the conclusion that a significant part of the impulse behind 'new thinking' as a whole was the leadership's awareness of the country's decline as a military, economic and technological power.

This argument must be carefully specified, since it does not in itself mean that the progressive elements in Soviet foreign policy have been merely a mask for self-interest, or that progressive Western ideas have not also played a part. But it is an argument which has persuaded a number of Western analysts – not without reason – and which Western policy-makers are likely to seek to act on, even if they have their own worries about declining US hegemony and the need to restructure Atlanticism in a sustainable form.

At its simplest, the argument is that the post-Brezhnev leaderships in the USSR gradually concluded that the Soviet system, or the USSR as its leading power, was in serious danger of losing the inter-systemic competition with capitalism. In spite of the USSR's achievement of strategic nuclear parity, by the 1980s the country was in a state of serious social and political stagnation. Lagging behind capitalism economically and technologically, the USSR was confronted by the prospect that the arms race would leap into a new phase which would expose and exploit its weakness. This last threat was symbolised by the Strategic Defense Initiative. But the fear was not so much that Star Wars posed a direct strategic threat by giving the USA total protection against nuclear attack, which would mean it could go ahead and attack the USSR with impunity: this was always improbable. The real threat lay in a more general range of scientific, technological and economic developments which would have applications for 'conventional' military forces as well as the nuclear arms race.

In these circumstances, Gorbachev's programmes of domestic reform and his active disarmament diplomacy can be seen as a well-calculated attempt to ease the USSR out of the most ruinous aspects of the arms race. They also aim to ease the pressure on the country and its allies by making the system more politically attractive and less incomprehensible to the West. Finally, they should ensure the system's longer-term economic viability through a combination of domestic restructuring and increased acceptance of the global capitalist system pretty much on its own terms.

I would argue that there is a great deal of truth in this analysis, even if for a variety of reasons it is not always easy for all parties to admit it. One can also fairly easily derive from it a Soviet policy of accepting 'unbalanced' agreements like the INF Treaty in the short term, in the hope of achieving longer-term objectives, and of proposing important changes in military postures in central Europe with a view to improving relations with an important link in the opposing system.

But it would be inaccurate and rather belittling to the USSR to see this as the whole of the story. The USSR is not a society in which the only impetus for change comes from inter-systemic pressure. Studies by scholars like Moshe Lewin, and accounts by writers like the *Guardian*'s Martin Walker, have shown convincingly how long-term shifts were taking place beneath the surface of Brezhnev's Russia. There was continued urbanisation, rising education, and increasing social frustration with a system which worked neither efficiently nor equitably.[9]

In addition, Shenfield's work has shown that the ideological underpinnings of Soviet foreign policy had their own capacity for renewal and revision, even if this occurred under pressure from the international system as a whole. Soviet commentators themselves have also confirmed something which began to show up from around 1985 on: that the alternative defence debate in Western Europe, among peace researchers and political parties on the left, was an object of interest to a body of scholars who were now encouraged to do research and publish on security issues. These scholars did not previously seem to have much access to military decision-making processes or classified data, and it is still difficult to determine what access they now have to these. Nevertheless, their existence has become increasingly apparent in publications from the USSR and elsewhere in Eastern Europe.

Perhaps the most difficult question in this area is how far changes in Soviet declarations in conventional strategy have been influenced by Western alternative ideas, as against more traditional security policy assessments. MccGwire argues the latter were more important. Much more research needs to be done on this, but I would suggest the two processes occurred independent of each other, and were only incorporated into policy declarations at the highest level under Gorbachev. One should probably avoid the temptation to attribute the changes to Western influence alone. The influence of the scholars in foreign policy think-tanks, who were very conscious of debates in the West, is revealed by the encouragement they received from senior political figures. But if MccGwire's account of the strategic basis of the reassessment is correct, then these scholars were simply lucky to be in the right place at the right time; they seem unlikely to have instigated the changes in their own right.

There was probably a further factor which has not received much attention. During the period of apparent Soviet reassessments, the USA's – and to some extent NATO's – conventional strategies were becoming more assertive and offensive, on paper at least. AirLand Battle, Follow-on Forces Attack, and the US Maritime Strategy may all have given the USSR good reasons to adjust its strategies away from the offensive to more defensive options. Indeed, in a surprising burst of candour, the Pentagon's *Soviet Military Power 1988* claimed that Western strategic developments had had precisely that effect on the USSR.

If my picture of the influences on Soviet thinking is reasonably accurate, a paradoxical picture emerges. I have argued that the offensive component in Soviet military strategy was not a myth invented by the right, although it was certainly not the cause of the Cold War; nor did it carry the political significance the right tried to give it. But in apparently revising this important aspect of Soviet security policy, Gorbachev seems to have been influenced by some extremely diverse and potentially contradictory factors: progressive ideas from the Western left; a belief that the socialist system was in decline; more specific strategic factors including, quite possibly, the increasingly offensive trend in Western strategy. The influence of this last factor may well encourage Western leaders to continue to take the same approach. This does not bode well for the future.

The Soviet Balance of Forces

More work needs to be done to account fully for the emergence of Gorbachev's 'new thinking' in security policy. By the same token, there are years of work ahead in following future developments within the Soviet political-military system and perhaps in East–West negotiations. All I can do here is sketch out some pointers for the future.

Until Gorbachev's December 1988 speech at the United Nations it was unclear whether any changes in Soviet strategy were being made unilaterally. Even before that speech, however, the projected changes were of major importance – simply because they were so radical compared with Soviet military traditions. It is worth remembering that no peace researcher covering alternative or non-offensive defence at the beginning of the 1980s could have expected that, by the end of the decade, a book like this would have to look in detail at developments within the Soviet military system. In this area, the chief concern of the first report published by the British Alternative Defence Commission in 1983 was to try to find ways to pressurise the WTO to reciprocate if and when NATO adopted a non-offensive defence strategy.[10] The fact that this chapter needs writing is in itself remarkable.

Having said that, one should also remember that the very radicalism of the projected reforms means that their full realisation will be problematic. In principle it is the CPSU which makes decisions on the resources to be devoted to the military and the direction of military doctrine. But major reforms of conventional strategy would have a much bigger impact on traditional military prerogatives than cuts in nuclear forces. It would be easier to make out a strictly military case for nuclear disarmament and impose a party decision from above – though there were reports in 1985 that some of the military thought Gorbachev's tactics in negotiating on nuclear forces were threatening to give away too much. If a major Soviet institution like the Strategic Rocket Forces saw itself in immediate danger of dissolution, bureaucratic infighting would certainly result, and we would then know better how far resistance can impede or delay major reforms. In fact, this instance would provide valuable insights into Gorbachev's reform project as a whole. The diffusion of power *within* the system is undesirable when the leadership needs to force reforms through an established hierarchy like the military.

A Soviet military professional might, nevertheless, be happy to go along with a greatly diminished reliance on nuclear forces. But there would still be room for considerable disagreement on the role of conventional forces, and the emphasis on offensive and defensive operations. The possibility of serious differences of opinion between the civil leadership and the military may depend partly on the factors behind Soviet rethinking. MccGwire's understanding is that the Soviet military were on board from the start, in an in-principle decision that a conventional offensive against Western Europe was no longer needed. If he is right, then civil–military differences would crop up only over implementation, not principle. If Jack Snyder is closer to the truth, Gorbachev is deliberately challenging a number of entrenched conservative institutions of which the military is just one, and the process of strategic reforms should be seen in the context of the overall reform programme. It would also follow from Snyder's account that civil–military differences might be more fundamental and hostile.

The evidence from Soviet military writings on doctrine and strategy between 1986–8 is ambiguous. Military writers already broadly agreed that the logic of strategy and the challenges of Western developments demanded more attention to conventional military technologies. Nor was there any sign of disagreement over the need to reform the Soviet economy, since a sound economic-technological base was a high priority even for representatives of the privileged military sector. But differences did emerge in the application of Gorbachev's term 'reasonable sufficiency' to conventional forces.

These differences were not surprising – the political leadership's original uses of the term gave no real evidence that its application had already been finalised. In effect, it was presented to the world before anyone had much idea what it meant. Dobrynin virtually admitted this in a May 1986 speech which encouraged Soviet scholars to do research on the concept and investigate the relationship between offensive and defensive strategies. When Gorbachev introduced the term, though, he fairly clearly implied structurally defensive postures for conventional forces. This was not always the case in subsequent writings. Military writers seemed more inclined than civilians to treat 'reasonable sufficiency' as a purely quantitative indicator of the *number* of conventional forces required, and to insist that 'sufficiency' depended on the opponent's capabilities.

But the division between military and civilian writers was not absolute. Colonel-General Gareev, a Deputy Chief of the General Staff, made some fairly explicit comments about plans to shift towards the defensive posture as the basic form of military operations. The technical journal *Voennyi Vestnik* began a series of articles devoted to the subject in early 1988, which seemed to indicate that troop training was undergoing some changes. The Defence Minister, General Yazov, published a book in late 1987 which endorsed the defensive posture as the basic form of operations, but seemed to settle for a formulation that continued to stress the importance of the counter-offensive:

Soviet military doctrine regards the *defence* as the main form of military actions in repulsing aggression. The defence must be reliable and stable, firm and active, and must be calculated to halt the opponent's attack, exhaust him, prevent any loss of territory, and achieve the defeat of the enemy groups' incursion.

However, the defence cannot defeat an aggressor on its own. Therefore, after repulsing an attack, troops and naval forces must be capable of carrying out a *decisive offensive*. The transition to the offensive will take the form of a counteroffensive, which must be carried out in a complex and tense situation of combat with a well-armed opponent.[11]

By the time of the 19th All-Union Party Conference in June–July 1988, the term 'reasonable sufficiency' seemed to have been rather pushed to one side in favour of the term 'defence sufficiency'. This was understood to encompass a high level of quality in military technology and training, an element which seemed to reflect some of Yazov's particular concerns. A number of the Defence Minister's articles and public interventions identified him as being not particularly interested in strategy as such, but a strong advocate of *perestroika* in the military. This seemed broadly to mean efficiency, making the system work without waste and to its maximum potential.

This emphasis on the military system's efficiency indicated a potentially double-edged aspect of Gorbachev's security reforms, which has caused some concern to Western establishment analysts. One possible outcome of reform might be smaller but more efficient, more conventionally oriented Soviet forces, with a somewhat but not radically more defensive posture in Europe. This may seem a desirable goal to officers like Yazov, though Gorbachev's own commitment to a serious shift to the defensive does seem firm. On the other hand, Gorbachev can hardly be expected to favour an inefficient military establishment and he will not endear himself to its leaders if his policies appear to risk that outcome.

This particular possibility should be set against another factor which I have already touched on – the emergence of a school of civilian experts on security issues, including some more outspoken advocates of defensive defence than can be found on the military.

This school of civilian experts includes retired military men and is grouped in the two established Moscow foreign policy think-tanks, the Institute of World Economy and International Relations (IMEMO) and US-Canada Institute (ISKAN). It will also presumably play a role in the newly formed Institute of Europe. As well as contributing an awareness of Western defence literature, these civilian experts seem to have played a major part in helping Gorbachev's leadership look at the USSR from the outside, through their sophisticated outlook on world affairs. They have presumably benefited from the increasing respectability of disciplines like political science and sociology within the Soviet academic community, although before Gorbachev came to power, work was being done which laid the groundwork for some of his policy innovations.

What is new is the high-level political encouragement they have received. Western observers have differed in the past over how much of Soviet security policy decision-making is derived from non-military inputs. But the public encouragement of these scholars is bound to affect the environment in which decisions are made, if not the procedures themselves. Gorbachev and Shevardnadze have also reorganised personnel in their foreign policy staffs.

Some of these civilian academics have been very frank with Western visitors about problems in their relationship with the Soviet military. But in the longer term, a more important consequence of their encouragement may be that once a freer, and fairly public, debate about security is under way, it will be difficult to reimpose restrictions on it.

In 1987, IMEMO published its first yearbook on *Disarmament and Security*, and in 1988 this was followed by a larger second edition on the scale of the *SIPRI Yearbook*. But as progressive Western organisations will not be the only interlocutors of this school, its future is not cut and dried. Its experts could become incorporated, not necessarily unwillingly, into the global 'strategic community' on its own terms – which may dilute the potential radicalism of their initial approaches. But when the second IMEMO yearbook was published, some younger writers who had not contributed to it voiced criticisms about the inadequacy of using only Western data in a Soviet publication, and called for more *glasnost* in foreign and security policy. Presumably Gorbachev and his senior advisers anticipated and approved this kind of development, which seems to promise that the debate will continue to develop fruitfully.

* * * *

With the constituencies in the recent Soviet security debate outlined, it is worthwhile looking again at how far foreign policy issues have emerged within the overall reform project. During 1986 and 1987 there was comparatively little public controversy over foreign policy questions. But by 1988, material was coming out which criticised some specific earlier decisions (for example the decision to deploy the SS-20) and offered more general critiques of Soviet policy in the Third World and Eastern Europe. By this time, of course, the Soviet withdrawal from Afghanistan was under way.

It may be that earlier no need was seen for a public debate on foreign policy because public opinion did not need to be mobilised to bring about reforms in this area, unlike in the economic or social spheres. To the extent that changes in foreign policy were explained in the press, the earlier material touched on points like the pressure arising from the fact that the USSR was lagging behind capitalist development. But it was not directly critical of past Soviet diplomatic practice. After the Nineteenth Party Conference, however, there was an exchange of views between Foreign Minister Shevardnadze and Yegor Ligachev. Shevardnadze called for pluralism in analyses of foreign policy. Ligachev, widely regarded as a focus of resistance to some of Gorbachev's more radical reforms, stated that international relations remained fundamentally based on class principles.[12] This approach had been almost entirely abandoned by Gorbachev and Shevardnadze over the previous three years, so Ligachev's rebuke to their foreign policy was sharp indeed.

What lay behind Ligachev's challenge? For Gorbachev, domestic and foreign policy are clearly closely linked – the urgent need for domestic reform makes external stability imperative, and the USSR's international decline makes domestic revitalisation all the more urgent. Ligachev may have been challenging Gorbachev on both counts: although not an opponent of reforms as such, he certainly seems to want to set limits. Ligachev probably considered the USSR's internal problems serious, but not serious enough to justify some of the more extreme marketising reforms and forms of political liberalisation that were being mooted. He also probably considered the country's international difficulties serious, but not bad enough to warrant giving away too much in negotiations with the West, or to seem to back down on Soviet commitments to Third World allies.[13]

The intriguing question also arises here of whether some of Gorbachev's remarks on the USSR's plight may have been deliberate exaggeration aimed at mobilising public opinion. This would have left him vulnerable to criticism from those like Ligachev, who were unwilling to accept that things were quite that bad. It is certainly true that the admission of weakness which was implicit (and sometimes explicit) in 'new thinking' did leave him vulnerable. But as I have argued, it had some basis in fact. Perhaps the crucial point is that if the basic impulse behind *perestroika* was to try to ensure that the USSR remained in some sense a 'great nation' – even in a more secure and significantly demilitarised world – a degree of exaggeration was necessary. Ligachev's own position was weakened at the September–October 1988 Central Committee Plenum, when he was put in charge of agricultural policy, while Gorbachev took over the Presidency from Andrei Gromyko. It seems possible that Ligachev's demotion had something to do with his exchange with Shevardnadze – although this would not necessarily help the reformers overcome lower-level resistance from others who thought like him.

Soviet Strategy and Conventional Arms Control

I have argued that although the significance of Soviet military strategy has often been misrepresented, it is more than a side issue as far as European security is concerned. The adventurousness of some of Gorbachev's security and disarmament policies from 1985–8 has ensured that a number of unanswered questions have been thrown up: about trends in military strategy, the role of Western alternative ideas, and the future of Soviet civil–military relations and security policy making. By the early 1990s we should have a better answer to these, but it is also likely that by then a new European forum for conventional arms control will be at work, the Conference on Armed Forces in Europe (CAFE).

These forthcoming conventional talks are examined in more detail in Chapter 5, and my comments here are related only to a possible Eastern approach to them. It seemed clear from early 1986 onwards that conventional arms control would become a focus in Europe as soon as an INF Treaty was signed. Awareness of this may have been partly behind Gorbachev's increasing attention to conventional issues from that time on. A shift in the Soviet attitude to negotiations in this area was first apparent in the Stockholm Agreement, concluded in the Conference on Security and Cooperation in Europe (CSCE) forum in September 1986, which allowed inspections on Soviet soil for the first time. MccGwire has suggested that this new openness to inspection is evidence of the defensive shift in Soviet strategy: with a more defensive posture, attaining surprise is less important and there can be fewer military objections to having one's territory inspected.

Nevertheless, there has been widespread pessimism about the prospects for progress in the new forum, and there is one cautionary tale to hand which suggests much of the pessimism is probably justified. The Mutual and Balanced Force Reduction Talks (MBFR) started in 1973, but 15 years later had still had made no progress in cutting conventional forces or arms in Eastern Europe and were finally disbanded in March 1989. It is also hard to see how discussions of doctrine will be incorporated into the forum, notwithstanding the initial meetings and discussions between senior Soviet and US figures that took place during 1988.

But the conditions in which the MBFR took place may not all still exist on the Soviet side. With the Soviet requirement for an offensive capability relaxed since the 1970s, military requirements can probably be more flexible in principle. A perceived need to maintain an interventionary capability in Eastern Europe may be more of a problem, but this need not in fact be incompatible with a less provocative posture towards the West. The vital question of Soviet intervention within the WTO relates more to the political disincentives which already exist than to any troop cuts or changes in posture which could result from East–West negotiations.

Until late 1988, although some unilateral shifts in the Soviet posture in Eastern Europe seemed theoretically possible, none had yet taken place. Gorbachev's December speech to the United Nations General Assembly, therefore, changed the terms of the European security debate substantially. It also put increased pressure on debates within NATO over post-INF nuclear 'modernisation' and conventional arms control.

The main points of Gorbachev's initiative as spelled out in his speech were a number of unilateral reductions in Soviet forces overall, and in particular in central Europe:[14]

- a total 500,000 cut in Soviet armed forces;
- withdrawal and disbanding of six tank divisions from the German Democratic Republic, Czechoslovakia and Hungary by 1991;
- withdrawal of assault troops and bridging equipment from units in those countries, together with reductions of 50,000 men and 5,000 tanks, and restructuring of the remaining divisions into defensive postures;
- reductions in Eastern Europe and the USSR of 10,000 tanks, 8,500 pieces of artillery and 800 combat aircraft (plus reductions in the eastern USSR and Mongolia).

Although the overall reductions in forces could be seen as consistent with an attempt to improve the 'efficiency' of the remaining forces, the heart of Gorbachev's initiative was its emphasis on restructuring in central Europe. The figures given did not add up, since six tank divisions only constitute about 2,000 tanks. But this suggested that the remaining units would have their tanks thinned out as part of the restructuring. Notwithstanding Western words of caution that the plan may just be to remove obsolete tanks, it does seem that if they go through as described, the reductions and restructuring would amount to a significant move towards a defensive posture in Europe.

Prior to Gorbachev's speech it had seemed likely that the new post-MBFR conventional negotiations would make very slow progress, and that this could give a welcome breathing-space to the Atlanticist establishments which were coming under increasing pressure as a result of Gorbachev's diplomacy. Since the reductions he announced did not go as far as NATO demanded, they did not in themselves ensure that the talks would after all progress rapidly. More significantly, though, the announcement exacerbated NATO's difficulties in maintaining a consensus over post-INF 'modernisation', and opened up new space for popular pressure in the West. The NATO establishment was left in some confusion over whether to welcome the cuts Gorbachev announced as a step in the right direction, or to make alarmed calls for continued vigilance.[15]

Nor did things seem entirely calm within the Soviet elite. At the same time as Gorbachev's speech, Chief of General Staff Marshal Akhromeev was said to have been transferred to 'other duties'.[16] Akhromeev had previously been seen as Gorbachev's right-hand man on arms control. But as some reports suggested, he may have resigned in disagreement, never having said anything to suggest that he favoured unilateral cuts in conventional forces. The reverberations of Gorbachev's initiative seem likely to be felt for some time in both East and West.

4

'New' and 'Old' Thinking in the Two Germanies

CHRISTIANE RIX

The two German states are the core area of military confrontation in Europe. If detente is to develop towards a real reduction in armed forces, the two Germanies will be at the centre of the process. But both the Federal Republic of Germany (FRG) and the German Democratic Republic (GDR) face contradictory pressures as they respond to the changing strategic context. The FRG is caught between domestic public opinion on the one hand, and US interests (which are served by some politicians in government) on the other. Detente is popular, but there is strong pressure to deploy new nuclear weapons. The GDR is happy with Gorbachev's approach to foreign policy, but uneasy that his reform programme is being taken as a model for domestic change in the GDR itself.

Like the USSR, the GDR emphasises the need for 'new thinking' in order to preserve the basic resources of life on earth. But NATO seems unable to respond. Since the end of 1986, it has been trying to develop a comprehensive concept on arms control to meet the string of new initiatives produced by the USSR and the Warsaw Treaty Organisation (WTO). There had been no substantial progress by early 1989, apparently because of disagreements on two issues: whether and how to include both nuclear and conventional weaponry in arms control negotiations; and whether and when to deploy new short-range nuclear weapons. West Germany is at the heart of these disagreements. Even among the leading figures in the West German government, there is no consensus about how NATO should respond to the WTO initiatives.

For some NATO officials, the WTO proposals challenge the political unity of the Atlantic Alliance. They think the proposals jeopardise NATO's 'flexible response' strategy and the credibility of nuclear deterrence. But the role of nuclear weapons in military strategy has been a constant cause of disagreement between Western European member states and the US since 'flexible response' was established.

While NATO has been eager to preserve deterrence, 'common security' has become a frequently used term in the context of 'new thinking' in the GDR and the USSR. 'New thinking' means a new general approach to international politics, and as such it also covers the military aspect of inter-state relations (see Chapter 3). The stand-point of the 'new thinkers' is that an end to the arms race is not only needed because of severe economic and social problems within the socialist countries, but also because there are only two options left to the international community as a whole: common survival or common extermination.

The idea of common security was first introduced by the Palme Commission report in 1982.[1] The West German Social Democrat Party (SPD) has since developed concepts of security partnership, or common security, as a new way of handling the co-existence of antagonistic systems in the nuclear age. In line with the SPD definition of the term, politicians and analysts in the GDR describe the current global situation as one where all countries face common economic, ecological and social problems equally. Indeed, 'common security' is now a widely known term in the socialist bloc – which could be a sign that perceptions of the international environment there have changed.

Common security is also seen as a *starting point* for a new way of managing and organising the international system. It is designed to establish a non-military 'peaceful competition' between socialism and capitalism, and a just global order.

The WTO has yet to implement – in terms of hardware – a new military doctrine. It will take time for it to change its military posture and organise for non-offensive defence. And to a certain extent such actions will depend on the response from NATO – on whether it joins in 'new thinking' on common security and disarmament, or simply continues to upgrade nuclear and conventional deterrence.

For West Germany, 'new thinking' is not just an external problem. The West German government is reluctant to disarm, for reasons which I will explain. But there is broad opposition to this position, from the SPD, the Green Party and a relatively sophisticated peace movement. At the same time, the conservative government itself has always been anxious to preserve the benefits of detente in its relations with the GDR. It has no interest in jeopardising this good relationship. Furthermore, politicians in the governing parties are increasingly doubting the reliability of the USA's security guarantee for West Germany.

Meanwhile, 'new thinking' will be the very basis of the SPD's new programme, scheduled to be ratified by the party conference in 1989. And practical steps already taken by the SPD and the East German Socialist Unity Party (SED) in proposing nuclear and chemical weapon-free zones show that disengagement in central Europe could be achieved, if the West took it seriously.

The socialist countries' proposals appear to favour substantial disarmament, they have to be met, and they seem to be in both Germanies' interest. But the government cannot afford to seem to question the unity of NATO. So it faces severe challenges about the exact nature of its security policy.

West German 'Old Thinking' under Pressure

After the October 1986 Reagan–Gorbachev summit at Reykjavik, Chancellor Helmut Kohl said that from the German point of view there are two principles for disarmament agreements: no wars must ever be fought in Europe; and Western Europe's security should never be detached from that of the USA. At NATO's Brussels summit meeting in March 1988, he again emphasised the importance of the nuclear factor in NATO's strategy.

Kohl's words illustrate clearly how his government regards the West German position as singularly difficult when it comes to its security policy as a NATO member. On the one hand, some aspects of NATO's deterrence strategy make West Germany feel particularly vulnerable. On the other, the 'old thinkers' in the government cannot see how an aggressive WTO could be prevented from attacking West Germany if NATO deterrents – particularly the nuclear systems – were not in place. Coupled with this is a conflict between the US and West Germany about how best – and with what – to defend their territory.

Official views of the role of nuclear weapons in NATO's strategy differ fundamentally in Western Europe and the USA. This difference is particularly marked in West Germany, where the government is afraid of a current US-backed tendency in NATO to shorten the range of nuclear weapons systems. 'The shorter the range, the deader the Germans', as the gruesome saying goes. Behind it is the fear that the USA may continue to accentuate war-fighting elements in its military posture. The more important short-range nuclear missiles become in US military strategy, the greater the risk for Germany, which is where these systems are deployed. In more formal terms, 'singularisation' is used to summarise German fears. It means that the FRG is in a uniquely dangerous position, exposed to the WTO's nuclear retaliation or even to pre-emptive nuclear attack.

But the West German government is still anxious to stick with nuclear deterrence. This is because the West German interpretation of NATO's strategy is that it should aim to end military conflict as soon as possible, because this would be being fought on West German soil. The aggressor would have to be compelled to stop before extensive damage was done. As far as the West German government is concerned, this would only be possible if NATO and the USA made an early demonstration of their determination to climb the ladder of nuclear escalation. So in this scenario it is vital to threaten the USSR with a 'full nuclear risk': that is, the USA must be willing to use its full nuclear strategic potential against the USSR in the defence of Western Europe.

In this context, the West German leadership did not at first welcome the INF Treaty, even though deploying INF missiles had caused the broadest protest in the history of the FRG to date. In mid-1988 the West German Minister of Defence made a series of statements about the Treaty, all of which reflected West German ambivalence to the pact. He welcomed it as a first step, but emphasised the need to preserve nuclear deterrence to counter the WTO's 'conventional superiority'.[2]

Having INF systems meant being able to destroy the second and third wave of Soviet forces on their own soil. And many German officials were afraid that withdrawing INF systems meant the US would be less likely to become involved in a war in Europe. They also feared that withdrawing INF systems would lower the deterrence value of the USA's strategic arsenal. Moreover, in their view, the Warsaw Pact's reported overwhelming superiority in conventional arms would only threaten West Europeans – and primarily Germans. So by their estimation, the more destructive the threat from NATO, the less the risk of being attacked. The more horrible a nuclear war, the less likely any war becomes. Such is the logic of the West German government's understanding of nuclear deterrence as a war-preventing strategy.

The USA, however, wants to avoid direct involvement in a war in Europe. It wants to reduce the risk of nuclear escalation – which would destroy not only the Soviet Union, but also the United States. Having INF systems targeted at the USSR from Europe was seen as a step towards reducing this risk, simply because they were not deployed on US territory. But since it became possible to produce smaller, faster and more precise nuclear weapons, the USA has gone a step further. It has tried to place more emphasis on conventional forces and miniaturised theatre nuclear weapons in its war-fighting strategy. The slogan, 'victory is possible', encapsulates this. It is the maxim of those in the USA who favour a combination of offensive and defensive systems – offensive, to fight and win; defensive, to survive.[3]

According to the 'old thinking' within the West German government, certain weapons systems are of the utmost importance in keeping the USA committed to and involved in European security. These include systems designed for selective first-use against targets deep in enemy territory – including Soviet territory if possible. Air-launched weapons which could be fired from German aircraft are also of great interest, as are sea-launched INF systems and ground-based missiles with ranges under 500 km.

The Autumn 1987 meeting of NATO's Nuclear Planning Group (NPG – the defence ministers of member states of the NATO military organisation) concerned itself mainly with the question of how to substitute for the INF systems. It did not find a solution – because the West Germans in particular were afraid of presenting themselves too openly as the main opponents of further disarmament. But no one was left in any doubt that substitutes will be found. 'Compensation' for the INF Treaty will probably involve bringing in new tactical nuclear weapons with ranges of less than 500 km, strengthening air- and sea-based nuclear forces and conventional modernisation (see Chapter 6). And the West German Defence Minister's comments on the INF Treaty in mid-1988 left open the option of modernising the remaining nuclear forces in Europe, particularly the nuclear artillery and short-range missiles with a range of 20 to 500 km.

Kohl made it very clear at the NATO summit in March 1988 that no agreement to remove short-range missiles would get West German backing. But he said he was against modernising short-range missiles in isolation from other weapons systems. However, by early 1989, with NATO modernisation well under way, Kohl had still to find a formula West Germany could publicly agree to for modernising these weapons, which would not spark a new uprising by the peace movement.

In the view of the West German government, the best way to improve security is to strengthen the European pillar within NATO through Western European integration and bilateral cooperation. Cooperation between France and Germany fits this approach. The formation of a Franco-German Council on Defence and Security and a joint brigade – both in 1988 – marked important steps in developing this cooperation. But playing the 'French card' in this way cannot be done without reference to the history of disputes surrounding France's role in NATO. In the 1950s and early 1960s, one element of these disputes was the USA's nuclear guarantees to Europe. They led to France's withdrawal from NATO's military organisation in 1966. Today, West Germany wants to re-integrate France more closely and with more German influence. Some people in other countries suspect that there are political forces in the Federal Republic who want to get hold of nuclear weapons themselves – certainly, such interests exist, although they do not play an important role in West German politics. In the first instance, though, bilateral cooperation with France is designed to pressurise the USA into not detaching itself from the European battlefield and to give Europe a more potent voice within NATO. France, as a nuclear power with its interests in arms cooperation and its traditional suspicions about the US guarantee, is considered a perfect partner. The French could be relied upon to back nuclear deterrence and at the same time share Germany's concern about its European deployment.

The Kohl government's contradictory position is made even harder to sustain by the domestic opposition it faces. The SPD claims to want de-nuclearisation and – for a start – nuclear and chemical weapon-free zones in both Germanies. Strong forces within the SPD are in favour of all foreign troops leaving German territory. The August 1988 party conference even decided to consider unilateral action if NATO members did not come to terms on disarmament. These would include, for instance, freezing the defence budget and halting some modernisation plans. Furthermore, the SPD has committed itself to giving up the whole notion of deterrence and establishing instead a non-offensive defence system – which offers no threat to the adversary but allows for efficient self-defence. This is in fact the logical conclusion of the concept of common security.

And no less a figure than Foreign Secretary Hans-Dietrich Genscher constantly repeats his view that NATO has to take the WTO's proposals seriously and get down to immediate negotiations on conventional stability in the Conference on Armed Forces in Europe, which started in March 1989. He is not the only one to believe that West Germany should refrain from modernising short-range nuclear weapons – which would place further pressure on the Warsaw Treaty Organisation – during these talks. He is, however, confident that as soon as NATO and the WTO come to an agreement on conventional forces there will be little difficulty in reaching a further agreement on nuclear weapons, since what NATO has seen as Soviet superiority in conventional forces will have been eliminated.

Some of the sharpest opposition to the government's security concept comes from the Green Party. The Greens do not just want Europe totally de-nuclearised. They also demand that the FRG take unilateral steps as long as no progress is made in multilateral negotiations. Unilateral disarmament was one of the Greens' main issues in the election campaign in January 1987. The Greens have also discussed a future strategy for a de-nuclearised, demilitarised and peaceful security system in Europe.

Although most Greens favour 'new thinking' and common security, some doubt whether the Social Democrats' concept would actually lead to an abandonment of nuclear deterrence – or of deterrence as an ideological system.[4] They want a more comprehensive strategy for a non-military relationship between East/West European, and other states. But in the first place, they criticise the SPD for not saying how in government they would respond to US, French and British resistance to abandoning deterrence. This is a question that SPD officials have so far failed to answer – but the pressure on the West German government is still high. It has been a significant factor in the government's delays over a public decision about how to go about modernising the Lance short-range missile.

'New Thinking' in the GDR – from Military Insecurity to Common Security?

The East German government was aiming to express independence and self-confidence on security long before Gorbachev came to power in the USSR. Accordingly, it welcomes Gorbachev's 'new thinking' – as far as disarmament and foreign policy are concerned.

Almost 20 years after the launch of Willy Brandt's *Ostpolitik* with the USSR, the Soviet Union sees the GDR as not only a stable and reliable Soviet ally, but also as a safeguard for detente and cooperation with West Germany. East Germany's importance increased in the early 1980s, when relations between the USSR and the USA were particularly bad. Gorbachev now seems to value any improvement in relations between the two German states.

Moscow has backed Honecker's policy of 'damage limitation' (*Schadensbegrenzung*) with the West, especially the FRG. While in 1984, the Soviets disapproved of efforts in the GDR to maintain detente and cooperation with West Germany – and prevented Honecker from visiting the Federal Republic[5] – they made no criticisms in 1987. His visit did, however, get some rather cool comments in some Soviet papers.[6]

And the GDR plays a leading role in supporting and promoting the WTO's disarmament proposals. In May 1987 the WTO proposed comparing NATO and the WTO's military doctrines, to analyse their different characters – how offensive or defensive was each? It suggested consultation on future postures to reduce mutual threat perceptions and suspicions, and to improve the opportunities for further confidence-building and disarmament.[7] In July 1988 the WTO's Political Advisory Council published a disarmament proposal from its annual meeting in Warsaw. It consisted of three steps. These were: to reduce both alliances' current levels of conventional arms; then make a further cut of 500,000 men; and finally, to introduce non-offensive defence strategies in both East and West.[8] Then in January 1989 the East German government announced a 10 per cent cut of its official defence budget by 1990 and a unilateral reduction of 10,000 troops.[9]

In clear contrast to the traditional way the arms race is run, the current Soviet leadership is striving for a situation where neither side can decide on its own how many weapons are necessary to stabilise East-West conflict. In this respect, Gorbachev's reforms are clearly supported by the smaller socialist countries. By April 1989, the GDR, Poland, Bulgaria and Czechoslovakia had all announced conventional unilateral disarmament measures. The new assumption is that one's own armaments generate more insecurity – because of the threat they pose to the opponent – rather than the previous belief that they guaranteed security. If this new thinking about armed forces and security is followed up, the legitimising foundation of the traditional arms build-up – which has always been justified as a response to the other side's new weapons – might be seriously questioned.

Turning away from the doctrine of a 'just' socialist war, and giving a higher value to non-military means of security and peaceful co-existence, could bring about a structural change in international relations as a whole. It would mean that peaceful competition would not aim to convert the other system or influence people there, but to compete in the best possible way to solve the severe international problems which affect every country, regardless of borders, continents and social systems.

Because of its significance as a 'detente frontier' with the West, the GDR will be particularly important for implementing 'new thinking' and managing its practical consequences. More than other socialist countries, the GDR could exemplify both the link between East and West for the new understanding of military strategy in Eastern Europe, and non-offensive management of the East–West antagonism. The GDR's influence within the WTO is definitely strong enough for it to play a key role in carrying out new political concepts.[10]

But the 'new thinking' is strictly limited as soon as domestic reforms come into the picture. It was remarkable that Moscow did not intervene in East Berlin's rigid handling of the independent peace and social movements and church opposition around the GDR in January 1988. East Germany's particular way of trying to differentiate between 'new thinking' on the international and inter-state level on the one hand, and the domestic on the other, can only be explained by its special situation as part of a divided Germany. Its economically much more successful neighbour has always been the yardstick by which the people of the GDR judge their own system.[11]

But it would be too simplistic to explain the East German government's handling of the January 1988 events as just a symptom of an inferiority complex. To be sure, this does play a role – because the government is not democratically legitimised and non-governmental organisations have limited opportunities to express themselves openly. But the government managed quite well despite this for some time. Now, however, the 'second Russian revolution' has been enthusiastically picked up by many in the GDR. In Gorbachev's own words, it is primarily a *domestic* project for increased economic efficiency – and democratisation of the system is a necessary condition of achieving that. This clearly represents a severe challenge for the East German government, particularly when its own peace and disarmament campaign is bringing improved relations with the other Germany.

A solution will have to be found for the problem of those who want to leave East Germany and start anew in the FRG, and those who oppose the East German government but want to stay and struggle for reform. It cannot and will not be found in suppressing the domestic opposition further, but will stem from reforming the country's economy and society. The economic situation is, simply, disastrous – which puts further pressure on a leadership with no political concept for future domestic development.

One very important challenge to the East German leadership was a paper worked out by the SPD's *Grundwerte* Commission with some members of the Academy of Sciences at the Central Committee of the SED. Published in August 1987 both in Bonn and East Berlin,[12] it deals with what it calls 'peaceful competition' between East and West; and calls for a 'culture of arguments on ideology' – basically, one which agrees to disagree. So the paper goes to the very heart of the idea of a peaceful co-existence of antagonistic social systems, and particularly the two Germanies. One particularly important question it asks is how far imperialism is able to act peacefully and cooperatively and, on the other hand, how far socialist systems can achieve reform and democratisation. The opposition in the GDR saw this as tantamount to a recognition of the need to reform the system, democratise it and enter open discussion with them. To the opposition, it meant admitting that reform is needed in the GDR too, and it opened a new space to discuss different ways to improve the socialist system. This was not, however, what the East German government had in mind. Its focus was on the inter-state relationship and the need for dialogue at that level.

So the East German leadership is currently in a unique situation. Not only is it under constant pressure from its neighbour's relative success and democracy. Lately, even its closest ally, the USSR, has begun to be seen as a model. By supporting disarmament and common security in Europe – which implies even more cooperation, interdependence and opening-up to the West – the East German government is seeking to compensate for its reluctance to reform its society. But it is becoming more and more obvious that the domestic contradictions of this scheme lead to explosive internal tensions.

* * * *

Although the advanced capitalist countries may be having profound problems, they continue to be economically healthier than the socialist countries. This, together with the internal economic and social pressures in almost every East European country, demands that the Eastern bloc find new routes to development. These include the difficult area of domestic progress. As a comprehensive political concept, 'new thinking' has yet to prove its worth by generating a will to reform. But there can be no doubting the credibility of the socialist countries' political intentions to reform, or their desire to disarm.

The GDR's domestic problems will not be solved by a further round of repression. Economic and social reforms are needed. Pressure for these is mounting, not only because of dissatisfaction in the GDR and unflattering comparisons with the FRG, but also because of developments within the Soviet Union. Even if the East German government supports disarmament and common security, it will not ease these domestic pressures.

The West German government is unenthusiastic about getting rid of nuclear, conventional and chemical forces. But there is strong opinion inside and outside Parliament which wants substantial disarmament, and which is prepared to trust the WTO's goodwill to move to a non-offensive defence posture.

Foreign Secretary Genscher is a powerful voice in this respect, though the majority in the West German government has stuck to delaying tactics – for instance, by repeating the need to develop a common NATO concept of arms control. Until this is done, they say, nuclear modernisation cannot be renounced and short-range missiles cannot be dropped.

The people of West Germany, meanwhile, want the chances for disarmament, detente and more security – which have not been as good since the end of the Second World War – taken up properly by NATO. The government would probably have to go to great lengths to get democratic backing for its approval of a further nuclear arms build-up. According to opinion polls taken in Summer 1987, more and more West Germans are in favour of unilateral steps. Their number has been on the rise since 1982.[13] The issue of security is unlikely to be decisive in the next elections in 1990, but the current government can expect some domestic political trouble in the run-up to them if it fails to start negotiating with the socialist countries; or if NATO does not respond convincingly to the WTO's proposals.

That election year could offer new perspectives for pushing forward disarmament. A new government may move towards common security. The SPD–SED proposals to create nuclear and chemical weapon-free zones could be a first *bilateral* step towards breaking down the concentration of arms in central Europe. The reduction of East–West tensions would be one certain result. The process would be aided by the effects of the reductions in Soviet forces announced at the United Nations by Gorbachev in December 1988; those cuts are to be completed by 1991. Also the fact that by April 1989, all the other East European states except Romania had announced or implemented unilateral reductions in conventional forces. Moreover, there is growing support in both European blocs for the idea of coming together to define common interests and participate confidently in talks about conventional arms cuts. European countries could even agree to hold confidence-building talks outside the inter-alliance nego- tiations, which are still dominated by the USA and the USSR.

But a new detente policy can be expected to go hand-in-hand with growing tensions within NATO, as long as the USA, Britain and France remain eager to keep and to modernise their armed forces – and their nuclear arsenals in particular. Dealing with this will be a major task for the West German government in the coming years. The change to 'new thinking' has already started in the minds of some people in the West. But there is still a long way to go.

5

Conventional Forces in Europe

MALCOLM CHALMERS

Since the 1940s NATO has based its strategy on the assumption that the Soviet bloc's conventional forces are clearly more powerful than its own. That this assumption is still the prevailing wisdom, though, owes less to the merits of NATO's analysis than to the political objectives it has served.

In the first place, it has justified NATO's heavy reliance on nuclear weapons as a deterrent not only to a Soviet nuclear attack, but also to a conventional invasion. The only alternative to this policy, according to some in NATO, is the politically unacceptable increase in defence spending that would be needed for the West to achieve parity in conventional forces.[1]

Second, Western defence ministries have exaggerated Soviet capabilities in order to justify more NATO military preparation and thereby satisfy a tendency in all armed forces to want to overinsure against an uncertain future. So convincing has this portrayal of Soviet power been that it has sometimes had the opposite effect – politicians have been convinced that Soviet power is so great that spending more on conventional forces would make little difference. Usually, though, the military has managed to argue that things are bad, but not that bad!

Third, the assumption of Soviet superiority has been used to justify a particular interpretation of Soviet intentions. If (unlike NATO, of course) the Soviet Union has clearly more forces than are 'needed for its own defence', then it must have other, expansionist, motives.

The Myth of Soviet Superiority

The assumption of Soviet superiority has always been questionable. A study by Matthew Evangelista of Stalin's post-war army has suggested that, contrary to the prevailing wisdom, 'Soviet troops were not capable of executing the kind of invasion feared in the West during the late 1940s.'[2] Detailed investigations done for former US Defense Secretary Robert McNamara in the 1960s came to the conclusion that the West had overstated the Soviet conventional threat.[3] And a 1979 Pentagon study, completed before the Reagan military build-up got under way but only recently declassified, estimated that:

NATO has already provided most of the resources ... needed to match the [Warsaw] Pact in total military assets ... As an indicator, NATO and the Warsaw Pact currently plan to commit equally-sized ground forces (combat manpower of 1.6 million apiece by M+30 [i.e., 30 days after mobilisation]) and tactical air forces (4,200 combat aircraft) early to a Center Region conflict.[4]

But although the image of a massive Soviet advantage has never been universally accepted, criticism has reached a new peak in recent years, as attention has turned towards the possibilities for mutual conventional disarmament in the Gorbachev era. Major analyses prepared for the Western European Union and the US Senate's Armed Services Committee, together with a string of independent studies, have severely criticised the official reliance (in public) on selective numerical comparisons.[5] As the International Institute for Strategic Studies warned recently: 'It is important to underline that a numerical comparison of the forces presented in this volume cannot by itself answer basic questions about the relative capabilities of each side's forces to perform their required mission.'[6] So far, however, the US government has refused to publish even a sanitised version of the much more rigorous 'net assessment' of the balance which it keeps for internal use. But if press leaks are accurate, this paints a less pessimistic picture than the one displayed to the public.[7]

More sophisticated analyses of the balance tend to present the West with a more favourable scene for a number of reasons:

- NATO military technology remains qualitatively superior to the Warsaw Pact's, and this is reflected in the more capable tanks, aircraft and ships now being fielded.[8]
- The quality of Soviet personnel is lower. Training is inadequate, there are high drop-out rates, and not enough encouragement for individual initiative.[9]
- NATO spends a higher proportion of its defence budget on support activities, such as communications and maintenance, than the Warsaw Pact. This potentially offsets any deficiencies in weapon numbers.[10]
- Official East–West comparisons tend to downplay naval and air forces, preferring to concentrate instead on ground forces. In air forces, there is rough numerical parity worldwide between NATO and the Warsaw Pact, and NATO aircraft are widely recognised as superior in quality.[11] NATO's advantage in naval forces is even clearer. As the USA's Defense Department acknowledged in 1988, 'the United States and its allies currently enjoy an advantage over the Soviet Union in nearly all important areas comprising the maritime balance.'[12]

- In most conceivable scenarios of a conventional war in Europe, the Soviet Union would have to rely heavily on the participation of its East European allies' armies. Despite (or perhaps because of) 40 years of Soviet-style state socialism, the reliability of these 'fraternal' armies cannot be taken for granted.[13] The Soviet leadership could probably count on its own troops' loyalty in a clearly defensive war fought on Soviet territory. But in a war of aggression against the West, much of the Red Army itself may prove less than totally reliable. Already more than one-quarter of Soviet draftees come from predominantly Muslim republics, and demographic trends will increase this proportion.[14] More come from areas like the Baltic republics, where the USSR is still widely seen as an instrument of Russian hegemony.

So overall it is clear that the USSR has as much if not more reason to fear losing a conventional war in Europe. Its numerical superiority in some weapon types cannot compensate for the qualitative weakness of its personnel and equipment, nor for NATO's greater economic and political strength. Even on rather pessimistic assumptions (from NATO's point of view) there was probably rough parity between the two alliances' conventional forces even before Gorbachev announced unilateral Soviet reductions in December 1988.

Stability

But rough conventional parity is no guarantee that a future war would end in stalemate, even if it did not result in nuclear catastrophe. Many other factors would determine the outcome. There is no shortage of wars in history in which a numerically inferior but offensively organised force seized the initiative and went on to win. In the successive German offenses against France and the Soviet Union in 1940 and 1941, it was superior strategy – plus, possibly, better morale and training – that ensured the Nazi control of most of Europe. The *Wehrmacht* at this time possessed neither numerical nor qualitative superiority over its opponents.[15]

So as a way of preventing either side from thinking rapid victory is possible, changes in the size of forces are in themselves of little value. The primary goal of conventional arms control is not (or should not be) parity, but 'conventional stability' – a set of force structures which gives little or no military advantage in striking first, and where the opportunity of a successful offensive is minimised.

A greater degree of this kind of military stability would help reduce the risk of a crisis developing into full-scale war, when neither side had aggressive intentions. This is generally thought to be the most likely cause of a future war in Europe. By reducing both sides' capability to take offensive action, it would help reassure those who are afraid that nuclear disarmament in Europe might make military aggression seem a 'rational' option once more.

How conventional stability could be concretely realised in both sides' force structures is currently under debate. There is growing support in the West for a policy of 'defensive deterrence' or 'confidence-building defence', in which NATO's conventional forces are designed to be as unambiguously defensive as possible. A number of European political parties, particularly the West German Social Democrats (who could be in government in the early 1990s) and the UK's Labour Party, are clearly sympathetic to the idea.[16] It has also generated widespread interest in the USA.[17]

Within the Warsaw Pact there is clear evidence that official support for 'defensive defence' – which has been evident for a couple of years – is being translated into practical moves. Gorbachev's December 1988 speech to the United Nations announced the decision to remove half the USSR's tanks from Eastern Europe, but a much smaller proportion of its soldiers. Together with the removal of assault crossing troops and equipment from forward-deployed forces, it is a clear sign that the Soviet Union has taken a major step towards reassuring Westerners who are concerned at its army's offensive orientation. It also implies that those Soviet military leaders who were resisting proposals for defensive restructuring have, at least for the time being, lost the argument.[18]

Yet – in marked contrast – the trend in the West is if anything towards placing more emphasis on offensive forces. The US Army's 'AirLand Battle' doctrine increases the importance of mobile warfare and the counter-offensive, and may make it easier to contemplate military action deep inside Eastern Europe. Large investments have been made in increasing the capabilities of 'Deep Strike' by both aircraft and missiles against airfields, garrisons and other targets well behind Warsaw Pact lines.

War games carried out by the Pentagon as part of an assessment of the 'Competitive Strategies' initiative suggest that the evolution towards a more offensive conventional posture will gather pace in the 1990s. Using the new 'Deep Strike' systems now becoming available, US wargamers could 'immediately disorganize a Soviet/Warsaw Pact attack, and then take away the Soviet strategic initiative with a NATO countertheater strategy in which air, sea, and land platforms targeted every key aspect of Soviet military power from the Elbe River to

Russia's Western Military Districts'.[19]

But military stability should not of course be considered in isolation from political stability. The Soviet Union's fear of Western aggression in Europe is linked to its own ability to prevent rebellion in Eastern Europe. It continues to be tempting for some Soviet leaders to blame unrest in Poland, Czechoslovakia and elsewhere on Western interference rather than on the inadequacies of the system it has imposed there. The possibility of Western military intervention is still used by Soviet leaders to justify 'fraternal assistance'.

On the other hand, more stable military structures in Europe could reassure the USSR about Western intentions and remove one of the major psychological obstacles to progressive political evolution in Eastern Europe. It could also minimise fears that the West might intervene if the political order in an Eastern European state were to break down. If this were to happen, it could escalate into a military conflict between the blocs. Concrete defensive defence would rule out the possibility of using military force instead of peaceful evolution to revise the post-war division of Europe.

Conventional Arms Control

One notable success in creating more conventional stability in Europe has already been achieved – the 1986 Stockholm Agreement on Confidence and Security-Building Measures, signed by 35 nations under a mandate from the Conference on Security and Cooperation in Europe.[20] By this agreement, countries give advance notification of military exercises above a certain size, and allow a limited number of on-site inspections on their territory on demand. It makes it more difficult for the Soviet Union to mobilise for attack – against NATO or an Eastern European state – without warning signals being given out. It is a useful starting-point for further measures to monitor and restrict peacetime military activity.

The Stockholm Agreement was one of the first clear signs that Gorbachev's coming to power in 1985 had opened up an opportunity for a long-term improvement in East–West relations. By late 1988, it had been followed by the INF Treaty, the substantial progress made towards a treaty in the Strategic Arms Reductions Talks (START) and the Soviet withdrawal from Afghanistan. The positive effects of the new Soviet approach are also being felt in the convergence of US–USSR approaches to conflicts in the Third World and the higher priority they both now give to global ecological problems.

This new climate has raised hopes that substantial progress can now be made in reducing both the level and the cost of military confrontation in Europe. The Soviet leadership's evident desire to channel more resources into economic and social development, and increasing pressure for savings in Western defence budgets, seem to amount to a common interest in reducing the cost of what is still the greatest concentration of military power on the planet.

The signs of progress were modest until the USSR followed up its professed commitment to a 'defensive' military doctrine with the announcement that in 1989 and 1990 it is removing 10,000 tanks and 500,000 men from its armed forces, disbanding six of its tank divisions in Eastern Europe and making further cuts in Asia. For the first time in decades, the Soviet defence budget may be about to decline in real terms. And the prospects for further cuts as part of a mutual East–West process seem more promising than ever before.

But despite this Soviet initiative, the leading NATO states have been trying to dampen public expectations of any imminent progress towards agreement on conventional arms. There is some justification for their caution, given recent history. The most recent set of conventional arms control talks in Europe – the Mutual and Balanced Force Reduction Talks (MBFR) – was unable to reach agreement after 15 years of work, and was disbanded altogether on commencement of the Conference on Armed Forces in Europe (CAFE) in March 1989. Started largely to forestall US congressional pressure to reduce the US troop presence in Europe in 1973, the object of these negotiations was to reduce personnel numbers in the two Germanies, Poland, Czechoslovakia and the Benelux. But they were unable to resolve data disputes – for example about how many troops there are in Poland. Because equipment was excluded from the draft agreement the gains to be made would in any case be limited.[21]

The agenda for CAFE is much more ambitious than the MBFR's. It includes all members of both alliances (23 countries in all); it covers the entire area from the Atlantic to the Ural mountains; and it includes both numbers of military personnel and major items of equipment.[22] But the prospects of an early agreement look slender. NATO's initial bargaining position calls for the Warsaw Pact to make reductions up to five times bigger than NATO itself. Many see the new talks – like the MBFR – as a means of reducing pressure for further nuclear reductions and/or US troop withdrawals, rather than as a real opportunity for large mutual reductions in conventional forces.

Given the possibility of further radical changes in Soviet policy, an agreement cannot be ruled out. But the odds are still against one being signed, let alone implemented, before 1993 or 1994. The problems of verifying a comprehensive conventional arms control agreement make the issues involved in INF and START talks look simple by comparison.

Even if limits are agreed on tanks and artillery alone, this would mean destroying or accurately counting around 100,000 separate weapons systems, each of which could be concealed in one of thousands of civilian or military installations.[23] If, as may happen, the talks attempt to limit numbers of armed helicopters, fixed-wing aircraft, bridging equipment and infantry fighting vehicles, the problem can only get more difficult.

Moreover, the Europe-wide scope of CAFE means that at each stage 16 NATO members must reach a consensus – each with its own vested interests, domestic political agenda and views on where the talks should go. The need for consensus not only slows down the process. It also means NATO will tend to take 'lowest comon denominator' positions and postpone all the difficult issues. As a result it could be difficult for NATO to adopt any bargaining position which is seen to require disproportionate cuts in the forces of one of its members – even if this position is sound. Once the talks get started in earnest, negotiations within NATO could be as difficult as those between the alliances.

Yet there appears to be little reason to suppose that the USSR will agree to a proposal demanding large cuts in the size of its army unless NATO also makes significant reductions in ground or air forces in return. The Soviet Union could always achieve the same political effect in the West by making significant unilateral reductions along the lines of those announced at the UN in December 1988. Moreover, being unilateral, these cuts would be readily reversible if the threat from the West was seen to increase. As such, Soviet military leaders could prefer them to an irreversible codification of much larger unilateral cuts – which is what the current Western proposals amount to.

Even if agreement is reached on equal ceilings for tanks, artillery, strike aircraft and so on, its value could be limited. Both sides have already agreed to exclude all navies from the talks, together with aircraft and ground forces based in North America and east of the Urals. Yet if these forces are left unconstrained, little money will be saved on either air or naval forces, and the result of an agreement might simply be to shift the conventional arms race into new fields – with little gain in mutual security. Most US aircraft designed for use in a European conflict are in any case based in the USA, and more could be moved back if required to do so under an arms control treaty.

Furthermore, thinning out ground forces without moving towards more defensive structures and doctrines could actually *reduce* military stability – because it could increase the advantage of striking the first blow. This may be particularly alarming as far as the Warsaw Pact's ground forces are concerned, because they have traditionally relied on strong numbers to make up for the poor quality of their equipment and personnel. If the Soviet numerical advantage is removed, Soviet military leaders will exert strong pressure for more resources to develop and produce equipment of Western standards, and pay for Western levels of training and Western levels of support. If this does happen – and a qualitative arms race replaces a quantitative one – there is unlikely to be much money left to make the reductions in the USSR's defence budget which its government clearly wants.

Priorities in Conventional Disarmament

For all these reasons, it is important not to think exclusively about the possibilities for a comprehensive agreement on large conventional arms reductions. Such a pact is a real possibility in the mid-1990s, particularly if we are optimistic about likely developments in US and Soviet politics. But to get to even this stage there will have to be much more mutual trust in Europe; otherwise there is unlikely to be the political will needed to tackle the numerous vested interests that stand to suffer from conventional cuts.

As yet, the political will for big cuts in Western defence budgets does not exist, despite the public support a transfer of funds into welfare provision would get. Governments' reluctance to rock the boat by questioning long-standing military commitments is reinforced by the powerful lobbies – arms manufacturers, trade unions, the armed services – which form when cuts are suggested in particular projects or programmes (see Chapter 7).

To create an atmosphere in which the public desire for lower defence budgets can overcome this caution, we should look at the arms control measures that could be agreed at the end of the 1980s and which could build on the momentum of the INF Treaty.

Reductions

• *A 'third zero option' removing all short-range ground-based missiles from service:* The first two 'zeroes' were the removal of intermediate- and shorter-range missiles under INF. Short-range ground-based missiles are ideal for pre-emptive conventional attacks, for example on airfields. NATO resists this option partly because these weapons are also nuclear-capable. But the West German government would be willing to support such an option as a way of avoiding a potentially damaging controversy over basing new NATO missiles on its territory. The USSR, despite its current numerical superiority in short-range missiles, is worried about the conventional and nuclear pre-emption capability of the new US Army Tactical Missile System (ATACMS). If some Western governments' obsession with avoiding any further denuclearisation could be overcome, a pact to cut out short-range ground-based missiles would be a valuable contribution to reducing the offensive element of both sides' conventional forces.[24]

• *A 'zero option' on the USA and the USSR's medium-range aircraft:* The USA's F-111s based in the UK and the USSR's Backfire bombers are the most important 'Deep Strike' weapons each side has, and could be used for both conventional and nuclear purposes. Their removal would significantly reduce the offensive orientation of the two alliances' air forces, and would prove a concrete first step towards a more stable structure of air power.

Such an option would be particularly attractive to the UK. With the removal of the SS-20 under INF, the Backfire bomber may now be the system the USSR would most likely use in a nuclear or conventional attack on Britain itself. Its removal would make the Royal Air Force's task in defending the UK significantly easier. At the same time, removing F-111s from British soil would address a long-standing Soviet concern about the offensive potential of US bombers based in Europe.

Last but not least, both the Backfire and the F-111 have been a source of continuing dispute in strategic talks between the super-powers – because they fall just below the thresholds that define 'strategic'. The F-111 can reach targets in the USSR, while on some esti-mates the Backfire can attack the USA if it is refuelled in flight. The more progress that is made in the START talks in reducing numbers of both sides' long-range missiles and bombers, the more important it will be to place limits on these 'grey area' weapons.

• *A ban or restriction on developing stand-off missiles on aircraft:* Because both sides have improved their air defences, it is becoming steadily more difficult for ground-attack aircraft to penetrate deep inside army territory and deliver bombs on their targets directly. But rather than use this as an opportunity to shift their air forces into a more defen-sive posture, the response has been to press ahead with a series of programmes for 'stand-off missiles' which can be launched from aircraft while several hundred kilometres away from their target. Deploying these missiles in large numbers in the 1990s will not only be extremely expensive. It also threatens to increase both sides' capa-bility to 'get their retaliation in first', destroying enemy airfields, concentrations of troops, bridges and so on in the first minutes of a war, or even in anticipation of one. Banning such weapons would force the balance of air warfare decisively towards the defence, encour-aging both sides to develop a more stable force structure.

• *Withdrawing a limited number of US and Soviet units* in central Europe as a gesture of goodwill and serious intent to agree more reductions. US Senator Sam Nunn has proposed that the USA withdraw more than two of its Army divisions from the FRG, in return for which the USSR would withdraw more than 13 of its smaller divisions from the GDR, Poland and Czechoslovakia.[25] Given that the Soviets are already unilaterally withdrawing and disbanding six of their divisions, Nunn's proposal suggests that disbanding one US division would not be unreasonable, and could make a significant contribution to the fiscal economies which the Bush administration needs.

How effective such a reciprocal withdrawal would be would clearly depend on whether both sides used it as an opportunity to make overall reductions, or whether these forces would just be redeployed elsewhere. Given suspicions that the latter could indeed be the case, it might be best to adopt a more gradual approach, allowing confidence in the process to develop before going any further.

There is no reason why first-phase reductions need be confined to ground forces. NATO might find it easier, in return for the significant cuts now under way in Eastern Europe, to combine a cut in the US Army contingent with dismantling some of the 30 or so squadrons of combat aircraft now deployed in the UK and West Germany. The former is likely anyway, due to budgetary pressure.

If this sort of initial step proved successful, there could be a move towards the long-term goal of removing all US and Soviet forces from foreign bases in Europe – a goal which Soviet rhetoric supports, but which has yet to turn into concrete proposals on the negotiating table. It would clearly only be possible to achieve such a goal if the USSR denied itself the right to intervene in Eastern Europe in the way it did in Hungary in 1956 and Czechoslovakia in 1986. So some Soviet leaders would see it as a threat to the cohesion of the socialist bloc. But the West has little to lose from taking Gorbachev at his word and testing whether this Soviet proposal is substantive or rhetorical.

• *Involving major Western states in reciprocal reductions:* The advantage of reciprocal US–Soviet reductions is that they involve only two countries, so can cut through the obstacles that the 23-nation CAFE is likely to encounter. But at the same time such reductions could backfire if it seemed that the superpowers were deciding the future of Europe without asking the Europeans about it. For this reason – and also because in countries like the FRG and the UK military spending is facing budgetary problems as severe (though on a smaller scale) as the superpowers' – the major Western European states at least must be involved in some way in the reduction process.

For example, Britain and West Germany could offer to dismantle some of their 'Deep Strike' aircraft squadrons (equipped with over 400

Tornado GR1s) as part of a package involving the withdrawal and disbanding of the 31 Soviet divisions in Eastern Europe, a cut in the size of the US Army in southern West Germany, and a withdrawal of some US Air Force squadrons from the UK and West Germany. A Western European contribution would help ensure that the initial phase of withdrawals was acceptable to the USSR, while at the same time actively involving three of NATO's most important members.

Confidence-building and Redeployment

Other measures which do not involve actual reductions in forces should also be considered:

• *An exchange of detailed information* on equipment and personnel numbers and deployment. The Soviet bloc has up to now been much more secretive than NATO about this. The new leadership in Moscow has proposed in general terms that such an exchange take place. But so far NATO has been very reluctant to test how far this conversion to military *glasnost* is genuine. And at the time of writing the USSR still seemed unwilling to publish basic numerical data about its conventional forces, for instance about how many tanks or aircraft it possesses. As a result, the Soviet Defence Minister still has to use Western sources to support his arguments about the balance of conventional forces.[26]

An immediate detailed data exchange could do more to build confidence about Soviet intentions than any other single measure. By making it clear whether or not each side had 'compensated' for initial reductions in one area by building up another, it would multiply the benefits of the limited cuts already suggested.

• *Establishing a corridor free of 'offensive weapons'* like tanks and mobile artillery on either side of the FRG's borders with the GDR and Czechoslovakia. This would build on a Palme Commission proposal for a nuclear-weapon-free corridor in central Europe, but extend it to some conventional forces. It would force those potentially offensive forces now deployed close to the border to be withdrawn or dismantled. Yet by allowing some conventional forces, for instance light infantry and barrier defences, it would encourage restructuring of conventional forces in a defensive direction.[27]

• *Agreeing to have permanent checkpoints and observers* from each bloc on the other's territory. Why should we not have NATO officers at every airfield and rail junction in Eastern Europe? And *vice versa*? The more similar measures are implemented, the more both sides will be confident that they could not prepare for war without the other side knowing about it. This would deter leaders contemplating aggression and reassure those whose job it is to organise adequate defences.[28]

Reversing the Arms Build-up

Reaching agreement on mutual reductions will be difficult, even on the limited proposals discussed above. Talking about reductions can end up preventing them, as it creates a tendency to hang on to weapons in case they are needed as bargaining chips. There is little doubt, for example, that the USA would not have agreed to reduce the number of its nuclear weapons in Europe from 7,000 in 1979 to around 3,000 in 1990 if these had not been the subject of East–West negotiations (although see Chapter 6 for an analysis of what this reduction actually means).

One of the most important trust-building steps would be a sustained reduction in defence budgets. Defence budgets are now static or falling in real terms in several Western countries including the USA and the UK.[29] Now that it seems the USSR will follow suit, those arguing that NATO countries should cut their defence budgets will have a stronger hand. This would gradually create a self-reinforcing process of mutual reductions without needing a formal treaty.

There are considerable problems in estimating exactly how much the Soviet Union is spending on defence, and it may not be possible to produce an exact total until full cost-accounting is introduced in Soviet arms factories.[30] Gorbachev's UN initiative in December 1988 should go some way to reassuring the West that spending cuts are under way. But the effect of cuts in troop numbers and older equipment could be increased if it were complemented by significant cuts in the rate of production of major items of equipment like tanks, artillery and aircraft. Figures showing these cuts could be made available quickly and easily. If the USSR is serious about reducing the share of its industrial capacity it uses for military production, this sort of initiative will be a very attractive option to the Soviet bloc.

Even if mutual reductions in defence spending can be started, these must be accompanied with a re-orientation of force structures and deployments towards the defensive. The recent Soviet moves to restructure forces in Eastern Europe seem to be a first step along this path. But other moves will be needed to provide an acceptable guarantee against surprise attack. These could include, for example, reversing the recent trend for Soviet air forces to place increasing emphasis on offensive operations. This would imply the static defence of borders was being stressed, instead of highly mobile counter-attack armoured formations. Such could be the role planned for those forces who are left in Eastern Europe but stripped of many of their tanks by the Soviet initiative of December 1988. It would certainly mean removing many of the hundreds of short-range missiles deployed in Eastern Europe, which pose a continuing offensive threat (nuclear and conventional) to much of Western Europe.

The USSR is unlikely to take all these steps unilaterally. But as Western defence budgets are squeezed tighter and tighter in the early 1990s, NATO too will have to find ways of making savings. People in the West need to ensure that their governments respond positively to Soviet initiatives, with concrete steps of their own to restructure NATO forces in a defensive direction. If both alliances were to reduce defence budgets and gradually shift their force postures to the defensive, the result in terms of cost-savings and increased stability could be much more constructive than a formal arms treaty can guarantee.

* * * *

The East–West relationship is now more relaxed since the days of detente in the early 1970s. But as at that time, the signing of a major nuclear arms treaty has not yet been accompanied by a slowdown in the arms race as a whole. So there is still a danger that today's 'new detente' could be as fragile as the 'old detente' in the late 1970s.

To ensure that the new detente is not just a temporary interlude in a continuing confrontation, Western governments need to be much more active in seeking opportunities for both nuclear and conventional disarmament. It is wrong to believe – as some do – that future Soviet policy depends solely on whether or not Gorbachev's domestic reforms succeed, and that the West should adopt a more passive posture until the dust settles in the East. The most important feature now is how far Soviet policy, in foreign affairs as much as in economic and political matters, is in a state of flux.

We should therefore not underestimate the extent to which a positive Western approach – which responds seriously to Soviet initiatives and makes constructive suggestions of its own – could help point the Soviet debate in a direction that would be in both sides' interests. Gorbachev's UN announcement indicated that those in Moscow who want to go in that direction currently have the upper hand. But their position is less likely to be sustainable if the West refuses to take its own positive steps. This chapter has suggested some ways in which both sides could seize the opportunity to begin the end of the division of Europe into hostile blocs.

6

After the Treaty – Nuclear Weapons in Europe

DAN PLESCH

The Intermediate Nuclear Forces (INF) Treaty has opened up unparalleled political opportunities for further nuclear and conventional disarmament, and for a new and more positive relationship between East and West. But these are as yet far from becoming realities. Both NATO and the USSR are still developing and deploying new nuclear systems.

The Treaty abolishes all US and Soviet land-based missiles with ranges from 500 to 5,500 km. Because of the way it has been presented through the media, it is often understood that *all* missiles between these ranges have been abolished. Indeed, the Treaty's name does refer to intermediate missiles without qualification. But in fact it focuses only on land-based missiles within this range. Both sides are still entirely free to build weapons with these ranges, so long as they are fired from naval vessels and aircraft. In addition, there are no restrictions on land-based weapons with a range of less than 500 or more than 5,500 km.

There has been considerable argument in NATO over which new systems it can get away with in the current political environment. Discussions have covered a range of weapons including Sea-launched Cruise Missiles, aircraft and airborne missiles and new Short-range Nuclear Forces such as artillery and missiles. NATO's Supreme Allied Commander Europe (SACEUR), General Galvin, has proposed a new gambit to solve the political problems posed by new deployments:

> At a breakfast meeting with reporters General Galvin said a study being conducted by NATO will recommend that nuclear artillery systems be pared significantly and that a smaller number of longer-range weapons be introduced. This will result in another overall reduction in the overall number of warheads.[1]

Galvin's proposal has been dubbed an attempt to trade in two pistols for a machine gun, and call it a reduction.

NATO's current planning covers Intermediate Nuclear Forces (INF), Short-range Nuclear Forces (SRNF – 0-500 km) and the fate of the warheads from the Cruise and Pershing missiles withdrawn under the

INF Treaty. To augment INF, the US F-15E fighter bomber, which 'will deliver the full range of precision-guided conventional weapons and tactical nuclear weapons will begin entering the force in the early 1990s'.[2] In fact, the first training squadron of F-15Es has already entered service in the USA. The conversion of some 50 strategic FB-111As into F-111Gs for deployment in the UK should be complete by the mid-1990s. These and other aircraft will be fitted with Tactical Air-to-surface Missiles. One type, the Short-range Attack Missile (SRAM) is planned to go into operation in April 1993.[3] The reportedly dual-capable (that is, able to carry either nuclear or conventional warheads) Modular Stand-off Weapon is intended to go into service in 1995. In addition, nuclear Sea-launched Cruise Missiles have been deployed since 1984. And new types of nuclear bombs for aircraft have been introduced in the 1980s.

In the SRNF category, new nuclear shells for 155 mm artillery will be produced and deployed from February 1990 onwards, pending congressional approval of funds sometime in 1989. The Lance short-range nuclear missile will be replaced by the Multiple-launch Rocket System – if Europeans agree to US deployment – by 1995. In addition, new neutron-capable warheads were deployed in Western Europe for 8-inch guns and short-range missiles in the 1980s.

The fate of the actual warheads on the INF missiles underlines the fact that the nuclear arms race is continuing apace. In 1988 the then US Defense Secretary Frank Carlucci explained that warheads were excluded from the INF Treaty 'basically ... at our request'.[4] According to congressional staff and US press reports, being able to re-use warheads from Pershing and Cruise would save both time and money in developing new ones. Up to $1,000 million could be saved. If Congress approves, Pershing warheads will probably be transferred to a missile for the new Multiple-launch Rocket System. This will replace the Lance short-range missile. The Ground-launched Cruise Missile warheads from bases like Greenham Common in the UK and Comiso in Sicily will probably be used on the new airborne Tactical Air-to-surface missile. But the warheads cannot simply be rebolted to new missiles. Some adaptation will be necessary. (Carlucci believed the USSR was less able to make this sort of conversion,[5] although the Soviet SS-20 warheads could fit the new SS-25 missile.)

These are NATO's plans to replace the firepower lost under the INF Treaty. The USA and NATO plan to deploy many more times as many missiles in Western Europe than the entire INF agreement negotiated away. These weapons will be able to reach the USSR. Hundreds of short-range missiles and artillery shells could also be deployed. These are, so far, excluded from any arms talks.

The precise mix of new weapons required by NATO may have changed in the aftermath of the INF Treaty, but the decision to move from large numbers of short-range weapons to smaller numbers of longer-range systems was taken back in 1983, at a meeting of NATO's Nuclear Planning Group (NPG – the defence ministers of member states involved in the NATO military structure) in Montebello in Canada. There it was decided to reduce and improve NATO's nuclear arsenal. Following that meeting, NATO has already, almost unnoticed, modernised its short-range systems and aircraft. A similar process is also taking place within the Warsaw Pact, although NATO retains a considerable technological lead. A new programme of the magnitude of NATO's has not yet been detected in the USSR.

The Politics of the New Nuclear Weapons

These plans will be carried out in a very sensitive political environment. The public reaction against the Cruise and Pershing deployments in the late 1970s surprised NATO leaders. This time, public opposition is widely anticipated by NATO governments. The USSR has already proposed – and NATO has rejected – an agreement to withdraw all short-range land-based missiles (the so-called 'third zero'). Such an agreement would be extremely popular in Western Europe, especially West Germany; NATO's rejection of it thus adds to its public relations task.

NATO has adopted a much more sophisticated public relations strategy since the popular protests of the early 1980s. When the programme was first decided in Montebello, on the eve of the Cruise and Pershing deployments in 1983, NATO presented it as a unilateral reduction of 1,400 nuclear weapons. It was only several years later that the 'Montebello decision' was publicly acknowledged as a major commitment by all the allies to new nuclear programmes. So far, new nuclear weapons (artillery, aircraft, bombs) have been introduced without public debate, fanfare or parliamentary votes. As far as possible they are being introduced gradually, invisibly, country by country.

Nevertheless, concern is growing, especially in West Germany, about the new short-range rockets and the air-launched missiles. One result of the controversy surrounding the deployment of Cruise and Pershing in the early 1980s was that it threw a new spotlight on short-range battlefield nuclear weapons. Opposition developed even among conservatives. As the saying goes, 'The shorter the range, the deader the Germans.'

In the next decade NATO aircraft will be fitted with stealth missiles, designed to be undetectable by radar, with a range of up to 1,500 km. In the Strategic Arms Reduction Talks (START) the USA has insisted that this kind of missile should be exempt from restrictions on air-launched missiles. Deploying these missiles may present a further political problem. Much more clearly than short-range missiles, they are seen as an attempt to undermine the political achievements of the INF Treaty, since they can rapidly and effectively strike deep into the USSR from Western Europe. In West Germany these stealth missiles – otherwise known as 'Pershings in the sky' – are seen as provocative by many. Many argue that they also present an extremely high risk of escalation in crisis and war. Any of these aircraft detected flying in wartime could seem to threaten an immediate strategic bombardment.

Reasons for New INF Deployments

There are several different arguments in NATO for new INF systems. One strategic argument is NATO's claim that Soviet air defences are continuing to improve dramatically, so NATO must equip its nuclear aircraft with missiles that will ensure a successful strike. Improvements are certainly under way, but Soviet air defences constitute no impenetrable barrier. In the public mind, the incident of Mattheus Rust's Cessna flight straight to the centre of Moscow in 1987 and the fate of the Syrian Air Force in the Bekaa valley at the hands of the Israelis will always cast doubt on their effectiveness. In any case, one of the primary nuclear roles for aircraft (and the new air force missile) will remain that of destroying these very air defences to allow NATO's air forces to break through them.

A more substantial political requirement can be found in NATO's desire to hit Soviet territory with nuclear weapons from Western Europe. Both sea- and air-launched missiles based in Europe are capable of this, but battlefield missiles are not. This requirement for selective nuclear strikes against military targets in the USSR was encapsulated in the new *General Political Guidelines For Using New Weapons*, agreed at the Gleneagles meeting of the Nuclear Planning Group in October 1986.[6] The *Guidelines* assume that it is practical to make a series of selective nuclear strikes, to which the USSR makes nuclear responses. First attacks would be made 'mainly on the territory of the Soviet Union'.

In a letter discussing the requirements of nuclear deterrence in Western Europe, Lothar Ruehl, a West German defence official, argued that the intention was not to substitute the systems withdrawn under the INF Treaty and thus neutralise the Treaty, but to retain 'acceptable possibilities, which are unaffected by this Treaty, for flexible and selective nuclear escalation options with regional nuclear forces'. Ruehl continued:

> For this purpose we should envisage alongside Sea- and Air-Launched Cruise Missiles of long enough range, fighters with Air-to-Surface Stand-Off Missiles. The number of such weapons would depend on the necessary targets, the survivability and accuracy of the carriers and on the necessary redundancy, to be certain of hitting the targets according to operative criteria ... emphasis should be placed on the dual capability of nuclear/conventional weapons systems.[7]

In October 1988, the NATO High Level Group (a permanent committee of senior officials from NATO defence ministries which reports to the Nuclear Planning Group) made a series of recommendations to the NPG. These included a decision to:

> Welcome continued progress by NATO military authorities and the United States in developing concepts of operations for developing SLCM [Sea-launched Cruise Missiles] and SLBM [Sea-launched Ballistic Missiles – Trident] in selective use, to be implemented in conjunction with adjustments to longer-range DCA [Dual-capable Aircraft].[8]

The recommendations were released to the press by researchers to whom they had been leaked. The jargon cloaks an aspect of NATO strategy which has never officially been made public. The decision affirms an emphasis on nuclear warfighting to be conducted through a combination of intermediate and intercontinental range nuclear weapons. To judge from these High Level Group recommendations, NATO is still committed to finding ways of making the use of nuclear weapons politically and strategically advantageous. The danger inherent in this line of thought should be self-evident.

Selective long-range nuclear missile strikes are also central to the strategy of *Discriminate Deterrence*. This is supported by, among others, Zbigniew Brzezinski (President Carter's National Security Advisor) and Henry Kissinger (who needs no introduction). It calls for highly accurate low-yield weapons which are 'politically usable' in limited nuclear war, especially in contingencies involving the Third World.[9]

These ideas fit in with NATO's long-standing *Tactical Air Doctrine*. The 1980 version states that 'in tactical operations nuclear weapons must be used with discrimination and precision; they must clearly indicate NATO's resolve to defeat aggression by assuring significant enemy losses while avoiding unnecessary collateral damage'.[10]

There are a number of less tangible reasons why some NATO leaders wish to press ahead with modernisation. Basically, some fear that the INF Treaty may be the thin end of a wedge holding open the door to the abandonment of NATO's policy of selective first-use of nuclear weapons. From here they envisage the complete disengagement of the US from Western Europe. So NATO's ability to modernise its nuclear weapons publicly becomes a crucial test of the resolve of the alliance.

A deeper concern is that further reductions in US and Soviet forces will make British and French strategic forces much more prominent, resulting in pressure to consider including these weapons in negotiations for arms reductions.

Another political factor is the accepted view that the risks a country takes in holding nuclear weapons should be shared between the allies, not placed solely on one nation. West Germany tends to think it is taking the risk with short-range weapons like artillery completely alone. It is often forgotten that other 'frontline countries', notably Greece and Turkey, also field nuclear artillery. The responsibility is actually shared by several other countries: those with their own nuclear aircraft, and those hosting US bases.

Sea-launched Cruise Missiles which can be launched from no specific territory provide a different solution to the problem. If sea-based weapons can fulfil NATO's needs, people are increasingly wondering why its member governments need to go to the political trouble of having any land-based weapons at all.

Reasons for Halting New Deployments

Some groups in NATO think it essential to deploy new weapons to show the credibility of NATO's strategy; many others see a strategy resting on the threat of both genocide and suicide as irrational and inhuman. They are unconvinced by the argument that as long as we have nuclear weapons in sufficient numbers, they will never be used. They rightly believe that a military strategy which can only result in the destruction of all concerned is no military strategy at all.

Public opinion and numerous political commentators see the INF Treaty as a watershed in international relations and an overture to the end of the Cold War. In these circumstances, people feel that the momentum of the Treaty should be maintained by pursuing further reductions in nuclear, chemical and conventional weapons in Europe. In the meantime both sides should freeze deployment as an act of good faith which would increase the momentum of the Treaty.

Instead of focusing on new deployments, then, NATO should

examine the minimum defensive conventional force levels which could be maintained as part of a 'defensive defence' posture on both sides. Negotiations should concentrate on removing offensive armaments like nuclear weapons, tanks and strike aircraft, and possibly nuclear attack submarines and aircraft carriers.

At present nuclear weapons not covered by the INF Treaty, and which are considered to be strategic, are excluded from any arms negotiations. So with the exception of the US Tomahawk Sea-launched Cruise Missile, which could be included in the Strategic Arms Reduction Talks (START), all the new weapons considered in this chapter are at present outside any negotiating forum. It is, however, likely that dual-capable systems will be implicitly discussed as part of the Conference on Armed Forces in Europe (CAFE).

From a more conservative point of view the new deployments can also be seen as both damaging and unnecessary. NATO already has a modern, capable nuclear arsenal. Some elements, like the Lance short-range missile, can be re-equipped to keep them in service rather than replaced. The nominal military advantage of new weaponry would only be gained at the expense of the likely political damage caused by a re-run of the Pershing and Cruise controversy. Moreover, European and global security would benefit far more from abolishing tactical nuclear weapons at sea, than from NATO deploying a few hundred Sea-launched Cruise Missiles.

START and East–West Relations

In the Strategic Arms Reduction Talks at Geneva, there are two major problems concerning Sea- and Air-launched Cruise Missiles. At the Reagan–Gorbachev meeting in Reykjavik in October 1986, Marshal Sergei Akhromeev, the Chief of the Soviet General Staff, was very concerned that a START treaty should include stringent limits on Sea-launched Cruise Missiles. According to Strobe Talbott, Akhromeev, who chaired the Soviet working group on arms control, said that reductions in ballistic missiles would be meaningless – and indeed unacceptable – if the USA could still surround the USSR with nuclear-armed Sea-launched Cruise Missiles.

However, Frank Carlucci, US Secretary of Defense in 1987–8, responded negatively to a suggestion from arms control adviser Paul Nitze that a complete ban on Sea-launched Cruise Missiles and other naval tactical weapons could be included in the START:

Secretary of Defense Carlucci and the Joint Chiefs of Staff vetoed the idea. Carlucci regretted that the Pentagon had agreed even in principle to put SLCMs on the agenda for START. He and the Joint Chiefs believed that the United States had to preserve the option of deploying ship-to-shore (or 'land attack') nuclear-armed SLCMs as a means of bolstering nuclear deterrence in Europe, especially now that American intermediate range missiles were going to be removed as a result of the INF Treaty.[11]

The argument for getting rid of naval tactical nuclear forces is, in part, that this would be a way to solve the difficult problem of how to verify any agreement on Sea-launched Cruise Missiles. This would help agreement on a new START treaty. But it appears NATO requirements are overriding this appealing solution.

The USA has resisted pressure to compromise on whether air-launched missiles with a range of less than 930 miles (about 1,500 km) should be included in the START accord, and here too NATO requirements play an important role. The US wants to protect further deployment of Tactical Air-to-surface Missiles and the new Short-range Attack Missile, SRAM 2.

NATO's new Intermediate Nuclear Forces therefore appear to be presenting obstacles to the conclusion of a START treaty. They may also create another problem. The USSR's new approach in foreign policy under Mikhail Gorbachev – known as 'new thinking' – has made possible such dramatic developments as the INF Treaty itself, and the unilateral reductions in armed forces announced by the Soviet leader at the United Nations in 1988. For the 'new thinking' to be successful, and for it to continue to produce a more creative Soviet diplomacy, it needs to register successes. If a START treaty is delayed, 'new thinking' itself may come under threat inside the USSR.

Stephen Meyer has argued that 'NATO's contemplation of compensating nuclear deployments in the wake of the INF Treaty – whether appropriate or not – undermines the credibility of the new thinking: the threat to the Soviet Union has not been controlled or reduced by the Treaty, merely redirected'.[12]

His analysis may give pause for thought to those pursuing the new deployments for narrow reasons of nuclear doctrine:

Professed Western interest in compensating actions to shore up NATO capabilities in the wake of withdrawal of US INF missiles from Europe has tarnished some of the new thinking's lustre. Even with significant Soviet concessions, it is argued, the West is finding ways to expand the threat to the Soviet Union. Western behaviour, and American behaviour in particular, can affect the long-term impact of the new thinking. This is because the most outstanding difference between the new thinkers and the old thinkers is their different perceptions of the threat posed by the United States and NATO. Western actions that can be perceived as invalidating the assumptions of the new thinking would be potent tools for those opposed to Gorbachev's security framework.[13]

The new missiles for tactical aircraft can also be seen in a wider context. There is a history of constraints on one type of nuclear system prompting escalation in another. The argument is that the 1972 SALT 1 agreement's restrictions on missile numbers led to more emphasis on multiple warhead systems and, since the treaty only affected ballistic missiles, encouraged development of long-range Cruise missiles. Similarly, it is argued that the fact that the SALT 2 agreement (signed in 1979 but never ratified) missed out Sea-launched Cruise Missiles encouraged their unconstrained proliferation. It is interesting to note, then, that when questioned about the impact of a START treaty on the tactical air force in Europe, the US Secretary of the Air Force chose to give his answer in classified session.[14]

Intra-alliance Issues

The greatest political resistance to deploying new battlefield nuclear weapons is in West Germany. In 1987, the Christian Democrats and Christian Social Union (CDU/CSU) who together form the majority group in the coalition government, resisted the inclusion of West Germany's Pershing 1A missiles and their US nuclear warheads in the INF Treaty. This attempt to obstruct the Treaty quickly backfired at the polls and they eventually conceded to US pressure, the NATO consensus and West German opinion and changed their position. But in elections since then the opposition socialist and green parties have continued to benefit at the expense of the CDU/CSU FDP parties. This is partly because of internal domestic reasons, but also because they have emphasised the need to respond positively to Gorbachev's peace initiatives.

The CDU/CSU parties are now pressing strongly for new talks encompassing battlefield nuclear weapons and conventional forces. There is a strong reluctance to continue deploying battlefield artillery shells and missiles, which in war would only kill Germans. With the West German election scheduled for 1990, some politicians see a need for an early decision to get the issue out of the way, while others (like Hans Dietrich Genscher of the FDP, the Foreign Secretary) want to delay this into the mid-1990s. The West German Army is reported to be in no hurry. But putting off the day may defuse political opposition if development of the weapons continues in the USA, and if the US Congress persists in its attempt to make Western Europe pay half of the development costs.

Faced with strong pressure for new weapons and higher defence spending from the USA and the UK, some West German opinion suspects a broader motivation, in which the aim is to try to sustain military tension in central Europe as a means of hindering economic interdependence between West Germany and the USSR. In addition, some West Germans look at the weak manufacturing base in the USA and the UK, and see the attempt to get the Federal Republic to increase its arms spending as a device to weaken its economy. Throughout the 1980s this sort of argument, drawing from analyses which show how high military spending weakens the economy, has been expressed by Western European politicians.

Southern European NATO members appear to be among the least enthusiastic participants in the nuclear modernisation programme. Spain secured the removal of US F-16s in January 1988 and is not part of any NATO nuclear programme, though nuclear vessels continue to visit Spanish ports and US Navy facilities in Spain include command and control installations. Greece has continued to negotiate on US bases and attach footnotes of dissent to NATO communiques – though if the conservatives regain power the situation may well change rapidly. There are persistent though unconfirmed reports that Turkey has refused to accept the deployment of more air-delivered nuclear weapons on its territory, in its reluctance to heighten tension in the region. At the Autumn 1988 Nuclear Planning Group meeting, the Turkish Defence Minister said that Turkey was not prepared to increase its nuclear burden.

In northern Europe, both Denmark and Norway have long refused to house nuclear weapons, but they tend to avoid criticising NATO's nuclear policies as a whole. And the Norwegian government was pressed in 1988 to agree to provide facilities for US Navy battlegroups in the northern fjords. NATO's plans are also generating controversy in Belgium, where the Defence Minister made public statements opposing NATO's new weapons in Autumn 1988.

The UK, Democracy and the Alliance

The British government now appears very enthusiastic about the modernisation programme – in marked contrast to its position before the 1987 election. The government was asked repeated questions about the 1983 Montebello decision. Many of its answers were factually contradicted by the US administration, the Dutch government, and the reality of modernisation.

When opposition MPs claimed the government had misled the House of Commons and the public over the Montebello decision, it protected itself by refusing either to accept the validity of official US statements or to comment on them. Now the position is different in two ways: first, the then Dutch Minister of Defence, Wim van Eekelen, endorsed the view taken by the USA and Britain's opposition; and second, the government has itself begun to refer to Montebello as the source of decisions on nuclear weapons.

There are two reasons for the government's change of stance: first, the election is out of the way. Second, NATO is anxious to prevent the new weapons from being seen as a substitution or circumvention of the INF Treaty – by presenting them as a routine modernisation agreed before the Treaty was signed.

Van Eekelen made clear that:

The Montebello decision also included a number of recommendations (a sort of programme of requirements) for Holland: introduction of the special mission teams for the 8-inch artillery, replacement of the Lance short-range missile by the follow-on Lance with greater range, and the introduction of new air-to-ground weapons with a range of at least several hundred kilometres (the so-called stand-off weapons for aircraft). No concrete decisions have been taken about this, though; the United States is also considering several possibilities in this connection. Moreover, the programme of requirements applies in principle to all countries that have a partic-'nr weapons system. The modernisation will therefore take place per weapons system, not in a particular sequence of countries ... The installation of stand-off weapons on aircraft does indeed fall under the Montebello decision, and is considered likely to affect Dutch F-16s.[15]

Explaining that the Netherlands would not have 155 mm nuclear artillery, van Eekelen stated: 'Montebello was in 1983. Since then Holland has in any case said that we would not carry out one of the points of the Montebello programme.'[16]

Van Eekelen's view tallies with the US administration's claim that the Montebello meeting endorsed proposals from the High Level Group which included specific recommendations for improvements to missiles and warheads. The missiles in question were at the lower end of the intermediate- and short-range categories.[17] Indeed, the Montebello decision is continually cited by the US administration in evidence to Congress when it is seeking funds for new weapons.

It is quite clear that as far as the Dutch and US administrations are concerned, decisions on new weapons were also made at Montebello, although some points of detail were left open. This sharply contrasts with the declarations of the UK government.

The British government did state in the 1984 Defence Estimates that NATO ministers approved the conclusions of the High Level Group's report to the Nuclear Planning Group, although it only referred to the part of their decision which focused on scrapping old weapons.

But a more revealing illustration of the government's stance can be found in its responses to a written enquiry filed in February 1985 by MP Robert Wareing. He asked a minister of defence, Lord Trefgarne, about 8-inch nuclear shells – converted neutron bombs[18] – which the USA has since deployed to West Germany. Lord Trefgarne replied:

> In the context of General Rogers' [then Supreme Allied Commander Europe – SACEUR] review of NATO's nuclear stockpile, no specific proposals of any sort have yet been made to Alliance ministers. You are therefore asking us to speculate about a situation which may not even arise. I do not think that would be wise.[19]

Trefgarne's letter was dated 26 March 1985 – on that very day, SACEUR submitted detailed recommendations for improvements in NATO's stockpile to the NPG meeting in Luxemburg. Then on 6 May 1987, following a series of exchanges in the House of Commons, Prime Minister Margaret Thatcher wrote to Wareing that:

> As the October 1983 Nuclear Planning Group Communique made clear, Ministers agreed at Montebello that the number of nuclear weapons in Europe should be reduced and that steps should be taken to ensure the effectiveness, responsiveness and survivability of the residual stockpile. In this context they identified a range of possible improvements. However, no decisions were taken at this meeting on specific measures to achieve this. Detailed recommendations for the implementation of the improvements were not submitted to Ministers by SACEUR until the Nuclear Planning Group meeting at Luxemburg in 1985. Lord Trefgarne's reply to your letter of 27 February 1985 was fully consistent with this sequence of events.[20]

Thus, just before the 1987 election, Thatcher's support for Trefgarne endorsed the position that as late as March 1985 the whole issue of nuclear modernisation was merely one of *possible* improvements which might not even arise, and about which it was unwise to speculate. But the Dutch and US governments thought specific decisions had been made.

Perhaps the most important decision arose from what is referred to in the Netherlands and other continental European countries as the 'Shift Study'. Its basis is a shift of emphasis from short- to longer-range weapons. It is this decision which is now used to justify new INF weapons. It also gave rise first to the NPG's 1986 Gleneagles revision of the *General Political Guidelines For Using Nuclear Weapons*, and later to the new operational concepts for using Sea-launched Cruise Missiles and Sea-launched Ballistic Missiles which were leaked to researchers in 1988 (see page 84).

It is clear that the Dutch saw themselves as being asked to agree to the requirements for the Netherlands, which they would then have to implement on a system-by-system basis as the weapons were produced in the USA. Two main decisions have to be taken in such a process. The first is an in-principle decision, made at Montebello when it was agreed that NATO required certain types of weapons with certain characteristics – like air-launched missiles capable of reaching the USSR. The second decision concerns detailed implementation: that is, precisely which nation will acquire exactly how many of a particular weapon. All the evidence indicates that the improvements decided at Montebello were definite, rather than merely possible, and that 18 months later, when SACEUR submitted his nuclear weapons requirements study to the Nuclear Planning Group in Luxemburg, it was untrue to state that these improvements might not even arise.

While any nation can opt out of the process, it is clear that as in industry, the final decision on managing the introduction of new equipment is of secondary importance, compared with the decision that initiates research, development and production by the manufacturer – which in this case was the USA. But the British government maintained the public position that this primary level of decision does not exist.

NATO's *raison d'être* is the defence of Western democracy. The management of the modernisation programme indicates that, at least in the UK, the apparent defence of democracy has become its manipulation. It is now clear that in October 1983 NATO decided to introduce large numbers of air-launched missiles, short-range missiles and nuclear artillery shells. Yet at the time, citizens were only told that weapons were being withdrawn. The public announcements of the Montebello decisions stressed withdrawal, and referred only in the vaguest terms to the new deployments which the NPG had discussed.[21] Particularly because this was the time when Cruise and Pershing were being initially deployed, much publicity was given to the fact that NATO was unilaterally reducing its nuclear weapons by 1,400.

Through the government's misleading statements, crucial information necessary to enable people in the UK to make intelligent choices was kept from them – but the US Congress and public had access to this information. The effect of such concealment has been considerable. One only has to imagine the condition of public opinion prior to the 1987 election if for four years there had been public discussion of the plan to introduce hundreds of new Intermediate- and Short-range Nuclear Forces without any attempt at negotiating with the USSR.

New Nuclear Weapons

This section is a guide to the new weapons being developed and produced. I hope it will function as easy reference as the debates unfold. Throughout the section, the figures I have used assume that both older weapons will be retired and that congressional restrictions on further deployments will remain.

NATO's Unnoticed Modernisation in the 1980s

Naval Weapons
The USA, the UK, France and the USSR have long deployed nuclear weapons on ships and submarines around Europe. The USSR has concentrated on deploying anti-ship nuclear Cruise missiles, and land-attack missiles with ranges of around 500 km. Western navies have emphasised nuclear strike aircraft flown from aircraft carriers. Since the mid-1980s the USA has also been deploying Tomahawk Sea-launched Cruise Missiles. Eventually some 4,000 will be deployed (758 of which will be nuclear) aboard one-third of the US Navy fleet: on attack submarines, battleships, cruisers and destroyers.[22] At present it is estimated that the USA has some 100 nuclear Sea-launched Cruise Missiles stationed off Europe, and plans to deploy roughly 380 by the mid-1990s – around half the overall total of 758.

Should NATO decide to transfer control of some of these missiles from US command at sea to the Supreme Allied Commander Europe, one option would be to allocate Spruance-class destroyers to NATO. The use of ships rather than submarines is likely to be preferred, since it is difficult to communicate with submarines. Ten Spruance-class destroyers could carry as many missiles as the entire Ground-launched Cruise Missile programme of 464 which the INF Treaty negotiated away. Only a portion of these weapons is at present planned to be nuclear, but it would not be difficult to raise this proportion.

Aircraft

NATO is continuing to introduce the highly capable Tornado nuclear-strike aircraft through the British, West German and Italian air forces. US and allied air forces are continuing to introduce F-16s in various roles. US nuclear bombs have already been updated. The new B-61 Mod3/4 hydrogen bombs are replacing older versions – the B-28 and B-43 bombs. The new B-61s have a more flexible explosive yield, including lower yields, which are thought to be more usable. This weapon can also be dropped from a very low height, through the use of delayed-action fuses which allow the attacking aircraft time to escape the blast. From NATO's point of view this increases the credibility of its claimed ability to penetrate Warsaw Pact air defences. The weapon is in use with US, Belgian, Dutch, West German, Greek, Italian and Turkish air forces.

Slipping in the Neutron Bomb

Army Missiles

The 'neutron bomb' is popular shorthand for small nuclear weapons which minimise the blast effects and maximise initial radiation: in official circles the weapon tends to be known as an 'enhanced-radiation device'. The USA's neutron bomb plans were the subject of a major political controversy in the 1970s. Though the controversy died down and neutron bombs were not immediately deployed to Europe as had been planned, they entered production and were stockpiled in the USA.

NATO has some 90 Lance short-range missile launchers in Europe; the missiles have a range of some 125 km. The launcher looks like a small truck with tracks rather than wheels. There are around 700 warheads for these, and over 1,000 conventional high-explosive warheads as well. The enhanced-radiation or neutron warhead for Lance is called the W-70 Mod 3. This weapon is designed to be deployed in a version in which components can be inserted, to turn it from a 'normal' nuclear weapon into a neutron bomb. The unassembled version, or pre-neutron bomb, is called the W-70 Mod 4. The Mod 4 has a much lower explosive power than the older Mods 1 and 2. The requirement for such a warhead lies in the need to be able to make nuclear strikes at targets which are on the battlefield but beyond the range of artillery, and to do so in a way which causes minimal collateral damage (that is, which destroys as few things as possible besides the targets). According to NATO sources the Mod 4 was deployed in support of all Lance units in the mid-1980s. Converting the warhead into a neutron bomb is understood to be possible because 'bottles' of radioactive tritium can be interchanged within the projectile with bottles of ballistically similar inert material.

Artillery

Since the neutron bomb controversy of the mid-1970s, the idea of nuclear artillery has become increasingly unpopular. In particular, many supporters of nuclear weapons find it hard to see how these weapons could be controlled in a crisis, when their physical control would be in the hands of dozens of individuals in frightening and dangerous situations. So it is rather surprising to learn that nuclear artillery has undergone a renaissance in the 1980s.

The number of nuclear artillery guns has doubled in the last few years. According to UK defence White Papers the number of nuclear artillery guns has risen from 1,100 in 1985 to 2,500 in 1988. The total balance of potentially nuclear guns is now given as 6,800 to 5,500 in NATO's favour.[23]

Some 200 new adapted neutron artillery shells have been deployed in Western Europe since 1985. These shells are for the 8-inch howitzers of the US, West German and Dutch armies. The shell (W-79-0) is a conversion of the neutron bomb. The weapon is designed to be convertible into an enhanced-radiation weapon by adding certain components. It is not known if these components are also stored in Europe. The USA uses a technical and legalistic turn of phrase so it can describe the production of components that can be assembled into a neutron bomb as not being *actually* a neutron or enhanced-radiation weapon.[24] In this way, it can provide its army with an enhanced-radiation capability while at the same time reassuring its allies that it has not deployed the neutron bomb. It is unclear how readily this work can be done in Germany.

General Rogers, former SACEUR, said in congressional hearings: 'These modern systems can reduce our reliance on greater numbers of less capable systems.'[25] However, as the political argument over NATO's nuclear systems gathers momentum, people should be aware that NATO has already carried out a substantial modernisation programme during the 1980s. The new weapons should be seen as a further increase, rather than a much-delayed improvement of an aged stockpile.

New Soviet Nuclear Weapons for the 1990s

The Warsaw Treaty Organisation is introducing a wide range of new nuclear-capable systems, from nuclear artillery to air-launched weapons. These programmes have all been under way for some time. Unfortunately, as the USSR still does not publish any details of its nuclear forces, the following analysis is based on Western sources and on the 'hearsay' evidence of discussions with Soviet officers and researchers.

Sea-launched Cruise Missiles

Since the mid-1960s the USSR has deployed dual-capable Sea-launched Cruise Missiles with ranges of around 500 km on ships and submarines. The International Institute for Strategic Studies estimates that there are 182 Soviet vessels carrying these in European waters. Two new missiles – the SS-NX-21 and a very much larger SS-NX-24 – are under development.

Aircraft, Air-to-surface Missiles and Bombs

SU-24 Fencers are equipped with missiles with a range of 475 km and other missiles (none of which has ranges over 90 km, and most of which date from the 1960s). In so far as the balance of military technology is still meaningful, the USSR is at a distinct technical disadvantage in this area. Its strike aircraft can carry a smaller bomb-load than their NATO counterparts and the missiles are heavier. So Soviet aircraft carry fewer missiles, and the USSR is less able to introduce this class of weapon in large numbers. The most modern of the USSR's bombers, the Backfires, remain unequipped with them, as part of unofficial understandings with the USA related to the 1979 SALT 2 Treaty.

In an interview with journalist Jonathan Dimbleby, Margaret Thatcher defended her support for the UK and NATO's acquisition of Air-launched Cruise Missiles with the statement, 'The Russians will be doing it, they will expect us to do the same thing.'[26] If 'it' is a decision to turn every fighter-bomber into an intermediate-range missile system, the USSR is physically far less capable of doing this than NATO. According to the US Congressional Budget Office, ten days after mobilisation, NATO will have 2,797 fighter-bombers against the Warsaw Pact's 1,249.[27] And studies by Joshua Epstein and the Carnegie Endowment say that for ranges of 200 miles (320 km) NATO's advantage in the tonnage of deliverable bombs rises to seven to one.[28]

Short-range Missiles

The USSR has long deployed large numbers of Short-range Ballistic Missiles. Three types were not included in the INF Treaty: the 300 km-range SS-1c/ScudB, the 70 km Frog-7 deployed since the mid-1960s, and some 130 newer SS-21s deployed since 1978. A total of 500 SS-21 launchers are planned to be deployed by 1992. These weapons also equip the USSR's allies, but only with conventional weaponry. NATO sources often give a figure of around 1,300 for Frog/SS-21 and Scud, including allied forces and those in western Russia.

Artillery

Three different kinds of nuclear-capable artillery guns are currently thought to have nuclear shells under production. These are the 152 mm, the 203 mm and the 204 mm. The USSR has almost 6,000 artillery weapons west of the Ural mountains, which are theoretically capable of firing nuclear shells. The extent of Soviet training for nuclear artillery roles, and the number of weapons actually designated for nuclear roles and supplied with nuclear shells in Eastern Europe, are unknown.

New US Nuclear Weapons for the 1990s

The figures in Table 6.1 anticipate the package of reductions and new systems described by General Galvin, the Supreme Allied Commander Europe. If it is implemented, it would allow NATO to announce a cut of 1,100 tactical nuclear 100 warheads. This would be its third reduction since 1979. The total then was about 7,000; in December that year, NATO announced a cut of 1,000. At Montebello in 1983, a second cut of 1,400 warheads was announced, bringing the official total down to 4,600, which the new package could reduce to the 3,500 estimated in the table.

However, as note 3 in the table indicates, official totals understate the nuclear arsenal available to NATO in and around Europe. As well as the USA's 600 Trident warheads earmarked for NATO, the USA plans to deploy 380 Sea-launched Cruise Missiles in the waters around Europe by the mid-1990s. Whether they will be assigned to NATO is not yet known. The UK's Trident warheads will be assigned to NATO, although they may also be used independently. France's nuclear forces are not assigned to NATO.

If the new package goes ahead, NATO will have removed well over 3,000 warheads since 1979, but it will also have brought in new systems to replace many others. The net reduction of 1,100 estimated in Table 6.1 allows for 2,100 new weapons to be deployed. It is a characteristic of modernisation that new weapons are more efficient.

Testifying on the 1989 Defense Budget, the then US Secretary of Defense Frank Carlucci stated that the INF Treaty 'highlights the importance of our continuing effort to modernise and strengthen NATO's nuclear and conventional forces'. His list of nuclear programmes that NATO had agreed to included new aircraft and nuclear bombs, a stand-off Tactical Air-to-surface Missile (TASM), new nuclear artillery shells and the ground-launched ballistic Army Tactical Missile System (ATACMS) as a follow-on to the Lance short-range missile.[29]

Table 6.1: Possible US Nuclear Weapons in Europe in the mid-1990s

Total in 1988:		4,600	
Removed:	464		Ground-launched Cruise[1]
	108		Pershing 2[2]
	100		Pershing 1A
	700		obsolete W33 8-inch artillery shells
	730		obsolete W48 155 mm artillery shells
	400		bombs
	690		W-70 Lance
Total removed:		(3,192)	
Retained:	1,000		bombs
	190		Nuclear Depth Bombs
	200		W79 8-inch artillery shells
Total retained:	1,390		
Added:	1,000		Air-launched (TASM/SRAM 2/MSOW)
	700		Ground-launched Ballistic (MLRS/ATACMS)
	400		W82 155 mm nuclear artillery shells
Total added:		2,100	
Estimated total:	3,490[3]		

Notes

1. This is a notional total, covering the planned total of Cruise deployment. In fact only 309 ever made it.
2. Again, this is a notional total. Only 120 were actually deployed.
3. NATO's figures always exclude certain categories of weapon. To this total, 380 Sea-launched Cruise Missiles, some 600 US Trident warheads assigned to NATO, plus British and French systems, should be added.

Sources: author's analysis, Stockholm International Peace Research Institute, Center for Defense Information, Natural Resources Defense Council.

Aircraft and New Missiles

In the aftermath of the INF Treaty, NATO plans to deploy more nuclear strike aircraft and equip its entire force in Europe with around 1,300 air-launched missiles with a range of between 400 and 1,500 km. New US deployments to Western Europe could include 60 F-111Gs (converted strategic bombers) and up to 144 F-15Es, which have been described as a 'wonderful nuclear delivery platform'.[30]

It is widely believed that Margaret Thatcher has privately agreed to the deployment of the new F-111Gs in the UK. A report in the *Washington Times* in February 1988 claimed that 'Britain would allow the United States to base as many as 60 more F-111 fighter-bombers on its soil to counter the East-West imbalance in conventional forces in Europe, a source close to Prime Minister Margaret Thatcher told the Washington Times. Mrs Thatcher has privately agreed to allow the additional planes ...'[31]

This claim was apparently supported by a later report in the same paper on the NATO summit in March. 'They had earlier passed the word that Thatcher will authorise the stationing of up to 60 more F-111s in Britain to take up the nuclear slack she fears is being left by the INF Treaty. She would make Britain the new European nerve center for flexible response.'[32]

As far as the F-15E is concerned, both the UK's Ministry of Defence (MoD) and the US Department of Defense (DoD) have refused to confirm or deny the destination of European deployments. However, a map presented by the Pentagon in 1987 alongside evidence to the House of Representatives apparently confirms suspicions that the aircraft will be based in Britain and West Germany.[33]

Missile Numbers

Given the expressed intention of equipping allied nuclear strike aircraft with Tactical Air-to-surface Missiles, and the emphasis placed by political and military leaders on the programme, it is important to make an estimate of likely deployment numbers. In testimony to Congress, US officials responsible for nuclear warhead production stated that 'The Air Force is taking the current GLCMs [Ground-launched Cruise Missiles] and considering putting them on to the Tactical Air-to-surface Missile ... [deleted for security reasons] ... It just happens to fit the problem of outfitting three squadrons.'[34]

Given the lack of firm figures from NATO, it is difficult to assess the precise numbers of air-launched missiles concerned. Estimates are notoriously problematic, as is illustrated by the INF Treaty itself. It was widely assumed, and stated by NATO, that there were 108 Pershing 2 missiles; in reality there were 120 – a discrepancy of 10 per cent.

Assessing the number of missiles on the basis of existing patterns of nuclear deployments, and taking into account additional deployments of F-15E and F-111 aircraft by the USA produces a figure of around 1,000 air-launched missiles plus 300 British weapons.[35]

While the individual estimates made in these calculations are open to challenge, the requirement of some 1,300 missiles seems reasonable given that a much larger figure is possible. Higher figures would be produced if other factors were considered, like reloads for second sorties, equipping more US and allied Tornados and US carrier-based aircraft, and providing F-15s with more than two missiles. On the other hand, a greater mix of missiles and free-fall bombs with the F-111E/F/Gs, and a smaller number of F-15s in Europe, would reduce the figure.

Missile Ranges

So far NATO has emphasised that the range of the missiles is no more than 400 km. If the range were to increase, NATO would be more clearly seen to be substituting for the lost INF missiles. In fact, there is evidence that the new missiles will have ranges in excess of 400 km.

For example, the *Washington Post* reported in September 1988 that the USA wished to protect 'future deployment of a new Tactical Air-to-Surface Missile and a new Short-Range Attack Missile [SRAM] said to have a possible range of 500 miles [approximately 850 km]'.[36] A revealing exchange also took place in a discussion of the Tactical Air-to-surface Missile (TASM) between Senator Sam Nunn (Chair of the Senate Armed Forces Committee) and General Galvin (SACEUR) in February 1988:

Nunn: What approximate range are you talking there?
Galvin: I would like to see a tactical – we have right now a Tactical Air-to-Surface Missile, but it is carried on a heavy bomber, it is not carried on a fighter. So a follow-on to that missile would be one that could be carried by a fighter which could penetrate air defenses if necessary. That extends the range of that fighter. I would like to see it extended as much as possible, obviously.[37]

The US Air Force, however, has declared a preference for the shorter-range SRAM 2:

The Air Force believes that SRAM 2 is the most responsive and cost-effective system that can be fielded to meet the CINC's [Commander-in-Chief] 'imperative' Initial Operational Capability of 1995. The characteristics and capabilities of TASM (and SRAM 2) include weight compatible with Dual-Capable Aircraft (2,200 lbs or less); launch envelope consistent with tactical employment; range of approximately 250 km; launch and leave capability; accuracy sufficient to achieve a 0.9 PD [a 90 per cent probability of damage] against certain European targets; warhead design and yields consistent with theater constraints; and size compatible with weapons storage and security system (WS3) vaults.[38]

Missile Types

There is much discussion of the different types of missile NATO may deploy. Individual nations and their armaments industries are competing for lucrative contracts, with potential orders running into the tens of thousands for the global market in multi-purpose air-launched missiles (for detailed examples, see Chapter 8). For these reasons it is important to understand the different types of missile being developed.

The eventual technology choice for the Tactical Air-to-surface Missiles to be deployed on NATO aircraft is not yet clear. The choice will be determined by a combination of factors: the political-military urgency felt in NATO to field a weapon capable of reaching the USSR from Western Europe; the cost of candidate technologies; the share of production income which will accrue to companies in user-nations of particular missiles; and the differing operational needs of NATO air forces.

By the mid-1990s it is possible that more than one dual-capable missile will be deployed with NATO air forces. The possible technologies include the SRAM 2, an extended-range Harpoon, the Israeli Have Nap, and a classified or 'black' US programme. In addition, there are reports that the NATO Modular Stand-off Weapon (MSOW) B is a candidate. At present, the US Department of Defense is seeking to pull together a wide range of programmes under its classified *Stand Off Weapons Master Plan*.[39]

Improvements in air defences are making it harder for bombers to get through to fulfil their missions. As a result there is increasing interest in a missile which can be launched from aircraft some distance from its target. The Modular Stand-off Weapon may fulfil NATO's needs. This sort of missile is being developed in NATO as a collaborative project between the USA and its West European allies and is expected to be operational in the mid-1990s. The 'modular' in MSOW refers to the fact that the weapon is designed to make it capable of carrying a variety of conventional payloads which can be fired over different ranges. The range of the weapon will vary according to its payload. The plan is to equip all NATO nuclear-capable bombers, like the F-16 and the Tornado, with MSOWs. Several consortia are already bidding for the project. With a modular design the conventional weapons could be fitted with smaller, lighter, nuclear warheads of around 200 lb, giving considerably extended range.

That the TASM, meanwhile, is to be a dual-capable weapon seems to be verified by its appearance in both columns of Table 6.2, which was presented by the US DoD to Congress.[40]

Table 6.2

THEATER NUCLEAR FORCES ...	CONVENTIONAL FORCES ...
Develop a Stand-off Tactical Air-to-surface Missile (TASM).	Develop MLRS, ATACMS, JSTARS, and new Stand-off-air-to-surface Missile (TASM).

The close association of the secret Joint Tactical Missile System (JTACMS) with the strategic Advanced Cruise Missile provides a further option for the long range of the new systems: 'The Joint Tactical Missile System is a Cruise missile that looks like a flying torpedo into which radar detection technology has been incorporated. It is just coming into operation; details of its performance remain secret.'[41]

The Multiple-launch Rocket System
To replace the existing Lance missile, which has a range of 115 km, the US administration has chosen a 400-500 km missile to be launched from the Multiple-launch Rocket System (MLRS).[42]

The MLRS consists of a container fixed to the chassis of a tracked, armoured personnel carrier, plus a separate ammunition supply vehicle. The container can fire a very wide range of missiles, including two long-range Army Tactical Missile Systems (ATACMS) or Joint Tactical Missile Systems (JTACMS) missiles; or two 'six packs' of missiles – each of which can in turn contain a variety of anti-personnel and anti-tank munitions. It is also reported that a chemical warhead is under development.[43] This configuration of two 'six packs' with a range of 30 km is the basic MLRS as it is fielded in Western Europe today, and to which a variety of new missiles and warheads will be added. The manufacturers claim each MLRS can be re-loaded in three minutes, compared with 15 minutes for Lance. The firepower of a single MLRS launcher is equal to an entire battalion of conventional artillery.

The Department of Defense testified before Congress in early 1987 that:

Army TACMS is generally considered to be a strong candidate for the Lance follow-on for at least three reasons. First, it would allow the Army to take advantage of development work already invested in conventional ATACMS, as well as the force structure planned for it. Modifications to the MLRS rocket launcher and procurement of the necessary missiles to make ATACMS dual-capable would not cost significantly less than developing and procuring the same number of an entirely new, nuclear-only system. Second, a dual-capable ATACMS would be more survivable than a force of nuclear-only systems, since all MLRS launchers will be capable of firing ATACMS. Third, a dual-capable ATACMS would be more attractive to allies, because they plan to field, and in some cases, co-produce MLRS.[44]

The likelihood of ATACMS being developed as the follow-on to Lance was further supported by Army statements to Congress, saying, 'We also need removal of the restrictions on further development of ATACMS as a follow-on to Lance', and 'ATACMS will be transported and launched from the MLRS launcher.'[45]

In congressional testimony the US Army has explained that the ATACMS can fire a conventional 800–1,000 lb warhead up to 200 km. Since modern nuclear warheads weigh around 300 lb, it would be possible for the nuclear ATACMS to have a much greater range. However, if the desire is to have a weapon of almost 500 km range, then it may be necessary to develop a new missile.[46]

According to the UK Ministry of Defence, NATO will acquire some 750 MLRSs, each of which is a twin-firing unit. The US Army has a worldwide procurement objective of 681 launchers by the end of the 1994 Fiscal Year.[47] Some 300 of these are understood to have been deployed to West Germany to date. There are reported to be confirmed orders for 198 MLRSs from West Germany, 57 from the UK (possibly rising to 68), 55 from France and 20 from Italy. It is also reported that the Netherlands has ordered 22 of them from the USA. Other NATO armies are expressing interest.[48] It is not known how many of the MLRSs would be equipped with a longer-range nuclear missile.

Artillery
The USA, Belgium, Britain, West Germany, Greece, the Netherlands and Turkey all field nuclear artillery. There are two types: 8-inch and 155 mm. Changes to 8-inch artillery have already been discussed (see

page 95). A request to Congress to produce the new 155 mm W-82 shell is expected in 1989: some 625 shells are likely to be asked for, of which some 400 will be deployed in Western Europe. The remainder will be allocated to other US commitments.

Like the 8-inch W-79, the W-82 is designed to be convertible from an atomic into a hydrogen device, with a very low explosive yield but very high radiation output. The W-82 will have a range of up to 30 km and an explosive power of up to two kilotons, compared with the 14 km and 0.1 kilotons offered by the weapon it replaces. This increased capability will permit a reduction in overall numbers, as former SACEUR General Rogers has explained.[49]

Before the modernisation programme began, the USA had some 900 8-inch and 730 155 mm shells in Western Europe. Congress has imposed a ceiling on the USA's total inventory of 925 shells. Assuming this remains in force, 400 new 155 mm shells will be produced to add to the 200 8-inch shells which have recently been deployed. The figures here and in the table on page 98 also assume that the older shells will be withdrawn since it is unclear whether they can be safely kept in service into the 1990s.

Other Systems

Although this section has concentrated on the main features of NATO's modernisation programme, the alliance's other weapons should not be overlooked. The USA, the UK and France all deploy nuclear-capable aircraft carriers, the US and Royal navies are equipped with nuclear depth-charges, the UK's Trident submarine-launched missiles will carry up to 600 warheads, and 100 man-portable Special Atomic Demolition Munitions are stockpiled in the USA.

Political Prospects

Neither NATO nor Soviet officials can view the political prospects for the 1990s with equanimity. On the Soviet side, the continuing tensions and problems in Eastern Europe associated with *glasnost* and *perestroika* will be exacerbated if the new phase of nuclear competition is not halted. The likely snail's pace of the Conference on Armed Forces in Europe dealing with conventional weapons at Vienna will increase internal economic pressures and consequently may produce demands for unilateral reductions.

Many analysts and commentators have pointed to NATO's twin problems of burden-sharing with the USA, and the need to take a politically dynamic position on conventional arms talks. In the view of the *Economist* magazine, NATO is staring at these problems like a dumb ox.[50] The introduction of new nuclear systems can only increase the political tensions in NATO.

The political and deployment agenda into the 1990s will present interesting opportunities to voters in NATO countries – if they are provided with the facts upon which to base intelligent choices.

A number of points remain to be clarified by NATO governments and officials:

- With the removal of some 400 Soviet missile launchers under the INF Treaty, why does NATO claim more longer-range nuclear capability is needed? What are the targets?
- The Montebello decision is increasingly portrayed as the cornerstone of NATO's programme to introduce nuclear weapons to Western Europe. Why then did so many governments not explain it in dealing with their parliaments and electorates?
- NATO is not willing to accept the Soviet proposal that all short-range nuclear missiles be destroyed. But what strategic purpose is served by NATO's intention to boost the number of its short-range launchers from 90 to over 750?
- In order to permit fewer warheads, will the power, range and number of nuclear guns have doubled?
- Will the forward deployment of stealth missiles on tactical aircraft lower the nuclear threshold? Is it not the case that a global conventional war would cause such chaos, communication problems and destruction of hierarchies of command that it would be difficult to retain control of strategic nuclear weapons and prevent them being used unintentionally?

It seems almost certain that all the proposed new deployments – artillery shells, short-range and air-launched missiles, and dual-capable aircraft – will severely damage alliance cohesion and political consensus. Indeed, it is arguable that a new consensus emerged from the turmoil of the early 1980s – namely, that nuclear deterrence is inherently unstable and should be relied on less and less until it is eventually done away with.

In this regard, one should consider the function for classical deterrence theory of large numbers of nuclear power stations and chemical plants. In wartime, their destruction – whether deliberate or not – seems almost inevitable. Even a non-nuclear war, then, raises the prospect of dozens of Chernobyls and Bhopals. Surely this should constitute a significant deterrent to war. What is the need for nuclear weapons?

The proposed NATO deployments are an affront to the possibilities of a new relationship in Europe. They betray public trust that the INF Treaty is the beginning of the end of the arms race. They subvert the democratic process in NATO countries, being decided upon and developed without so much as informing the public. They represent a barely rational 'born again' affirmation of fighting limited nuclear wars, and have an excellent chance of undermining the internal position of Mikhail Gorbachev. In short, there is little to recommend them.

7

The Power of Star Wars*

MARIO PIANTA

How do you describe the economy of a superpower that is increasingly inefficient at home and increasingly assertive abroad? An economy that is far from able to produce all the goods it consumes, sinking into deficits and debts, but despite restricting its extravagance, is still determined to maintain exceptionally high levels of military spending and production? And which persists in using this as a tool to preserve its international power and control over its allies' economic decision-making?

This may sound like a profile of the USSR – with a 'command' economy serving first of all its position as a military superpower and leader of the Eastern bloc. But it is as applicable to the United States at the end of the Reagan era. Here an illusion of restored growth and leadership has given way to major economic problems at home and strains with its allies abroad.

In the 1980s the United States has devoted two trillion dollars to military spending, engaged in the greatest arms race in history, specialised its economy and industrial base in military production, concentrated research and development on defence, and launched the Strategic Defense Initiative (SDI) as a symbol and culmination of all these policies. The domestic side of the story is well known, but less attention has been paid to its international dimension. After decades of slow US economic and political decline – relative to its West European and Japanese allies – the USA's strategy has been to restore US hegemony, using political and military power to regain control over the international economy and leadership over the West.

A wide range of initiatives have been developed with this aim. The most important, the Strategic Defense Initiative (widely known as 'Star Wars') is the largest research project ever developed by a Western government. As a military programme, Star Wars has aimed to restore US military superiority over the USSR. But as a technological strategy, the project was developed to re-establish US control over the direction of technical change, to set the ground for the competition with

---

*Revised and reprinted with kind permission of *Socialist Review*, Berkeley, CA.

Western Europe and Japan. Star Wars brought with it an active industrial policy of stronger national import/export regulations and tighter
government controls on foreign acquisitions of US high-tech industries.

Many commentators seem to have thought that the end of Reagan's
presidency also meant the end of Star Wars. A complete about-turn is
hardly likely. It is impossible to delete at a stroke such a big research
and development programme. Star Wars is simply too resilient; it has
too many supporters in the arms industry, the community of strategic
experts and Congress. It may be cut back, have its priorities re-ordered
and get a new name, but the US military bureaucracy has never easiy
allowed such large programmes to be scrapped. Moreover, if the Bush
administration sees Star Wars' potential in the technology race, there
will be a political as well as a bureaucratic reason for keeping SDI
going.

Fantasy – Technological Power

The international technological landscape has changed dramatically in
the last few decades. The USA's loss of leadership in a broad set of
advanced technologies has become evident, while Japan and Western
Europe have caught up and gone on, to develop new capabilities at the
'technological frontier'. Now they devote a greater share of their
resources than the US to commercial research and development. They
have shown a remarkable ability to apply these advances to their own
industrial base, as innovations in processes and products, and an
increasing interest in the new directions of technological development.[1]

Against this background, a national technology strategy cannot
conceivably aim for an overall leadership across the board of sectors
and industries. Instead it must try to set the national economy in the
best possible position within the international division of labour,
selecting those areas and sectors where there is greatest strength and
which stand to bring the greatest advantage.

In the case of the USA in the 1980s, this has meant focusing technological initiatives on areas where the US already had the greatest
comparative technological advantage over Europe and Japan, and
where it could make the greatest political use of this. Within a wide
range of the new technologies – microelectronics, computers, telecommunications, optics, space, materials, biotechnology – the US
government has focused its efforts on 'strategic' areas, defined in terms
of their importance for 'national security', and on military applications. In fact, military technology is perhaps the area where the US has

the greatest specialisation in fields where other countries are often barely present. Here, the US has developed a set of institutions with a long tradition of funding and directing technological change. It can also use the outcome of such innovations – new weapons and military strategies – to enhance its power in international relations.

Star Wars exemplifies this mix of technology, economics and politics. The launch of the programme renewed US faith in technology, in *American* technology, and in its ability to solve complex political problems like the nuclear threat. Such a major initiative seemed set to revive the USA's technological leadership, defined a new direction for technical change and laid out new ground for economic competition between the more advanced countries. It also increased the military and political power of the US, both in the East–West confrontation and in Western relations. For the government of a country in economic decline, with its hegemony eroded, this strategy may have understandably seemed a perfect way to restore it to leadership.

Star Wars is not the only aspect of this strategy. Other current US policies have in the same way considered technology as a weapon in international relations, capable of re-establishing US control over 'strategic' know-how. The US has restricted international technology transfers – in particular to the Eastern bloc – giving the US Defense Department the power to authorise (or veto) foreign sales of a long list of high-technology products, and pressing both NATO and neutral countries in Western Europe to enforce the same restrictions. US government intervention and protection in the semiconductor industry is one example of the same strategy of resisting the penetration of foreign producers, particularly Japanese acquisitions of US firms. The tendency towards greater political control and more explicit government intervention in industry and technology was also stressed by the congressional approval of the 1988 Trade Bill.[2]

SDI, however, is more than just one element among many in the overall effort. Sitting at the intersection of nuclear, strategic, international power politics and high technology, it epitomises the technological route to restoring US hegemony. What was often left out of the debate about Star Wars was that, as an instrument of power, it is as much a technological as a military strategy.

Within the US, this strategy has been part of the rapid expansion of the military economy and of defence-oriented research, with 'national security' objectives prevailing over the bid for US industry's international competitiveness. In fact, Star Wars technology has brought to a head the divergence between military research and civilian innovation that has contributed so much to the deterioration in the USA's technological performance.[3] These facts also suggest that the current race for high military technology is unlikely to contribute to a new 'long wave' of world economic growth, with the US leading a new cycle of world-wide accumulation and rebuilding its hegemony on an economic basis. Both the technological and the institutional factors that have been associated in the past with the emergence of a 'long wave' seem now to be missing. The 'strategic technologies' on which Star Wars focuses are unlikely to play the same sort of role as that played by the mechanical, chemical and energy technologies associated with the rise of the US economy at the beginning of this century.

Using Star Wars as a technological strategy, therefore, does not seem a sound basis for restoring technological advance and economic growth and reversing the US's decline. However, to succeed, such a strategy does not need to achieve a renewed, sustained expansion of the world economy. It is enough that Western Europe and Japan accept the combination of political, military and technological pressure and follow the US into military oriented research, an increasingly militarised economy and a 'Star Wars' type of technology. Because this is the competition that Europe and Japan are most likely to lose, giving US hegemony a new lease of life.

The US strategy has seriously affected Western relations. It was conceived in a period of renewed Cold War, when the value of military power within the Western alliance had suddenly increased. So it inflated the value of military technology exactly when the US was losing ground to Western Europe and Japan in civilian technology. This has produced deepening contradictions, as the growing US reliance on military power also accelerated the erosion of its economic strength.

As dangerous as it is for international peace and the stability of the world economy, the strategy has scored some successes in recovering in political terms what the USA had lost on the economic ground. In its relations within the Western alliance, the US position has shifted from an undisputed political, economic and technological leadership to an increasingly disputed international role that largely relies on US military might. It is remarkable that in many ways both the domestic and international transformations of the US political economy prompt the observer to see growing parallels with Soviet power over the Eastern bloc.

Reality – Deceit and Profit

Six years after the launch of Star Wars, the profile of the programme is a long way off what was promised at the outset. Its aim has shifted from providing an 'impenetrable shield' over the USA (and its allies) to focus instead on the 'early deployment' of limited anti-missile systems.[4] The technologies developed within SDI are much less innovative and 'futuristic' than anticipated, and most funds are now devoted to developing and testing partial systems using older technologies.[5]

In addition, the political tide has turned against Star Wars. As Congress slowed down the expansion of the US military budget in Reagan's last three years in office, it cut allocations for SDI funds. Partly this simply reflected the general process of tightening the purse strings; partly it reflected the specific doubts about SDI's technical feasibility and strategic desirability. Thus while for the three Fiscal Years 1986–8 the administration wanted $14.9 billion for SDI, it got $10.4 billion; while it wanted SDI funding to grow in that time by 50 per cent, it was granted an increase of 30 per cent. These are still enormous sums and a fast rate of growth, but well short of what the administration sought.

Star Wars also lost steam in the new atmosphere of detente in the last two years of Reagan's presidency. Now he is out of office, there will be further pressure on his pet project. There is general consensus in Congress that military spending must at least be stabilised, and strong opinion that it should be reduced. Star Wars seems a likely candidate for cuts, not least because President Bush is widely seen as less of an SDI enthusiast than Reagan – perhaps rightly, since he lacks Reagan's personal investment in the project.

Yet the Bush administration may well give SDI a new start. Although it will probably be less grandiose, the programme is likely to remain a priority in US military and research strategies. The institutional momentum of SDI should not be underestimated. Star Wars ideas are already established in the world of strategic thinking, and Star Wars contracts are a growing interest of the US military industry. Finally, the example of past US military programmes – like the B-1 bomber, which had been cancelled by President Carter and is now operational – has shown how resilient military research programmes can be in the face of changing administrations' priorities.

Discriminate Deterrence, the Presidential Commission on Integrated Long-Term Strategy's 1988 report, argued that 'to help deter nuclear attack and to make it safer to reduce offensive arms we need strategic defense'. It went on to say that the US 'should recognize that a limited initial deployment of ballistic missile defenses can be of value for several important contingencies, and we should pursue research and development aimed at such initial capabilities'.[6]

SDI is also a major economic reality. By the end of 1987 appropriations for SDI totalled between $12 billion and $14 billion. The funds

Table 7.1: Top 20 SDI Contractors, Fiscal Year 1983–6

Company	Value of contracts ($ thousand)	Share of total SDI contracts (per cent)
Lockheed[a]	720,961	9.8
General Motors	612,698	8.4
Boeing	373,697	5.1
TRW	373,117	5.1
DOE Lawrence Livermore Nat. Lab.[a]	366,685	5.0
EG&G[a]	360,300	4.9
McDonnell Douglas	338,224	4.6
MIT Lincoln Lab	327,542	4.5
DOE Los Alamos Nat. Lab.[a]	285,588	3.9
General Electric	260,797	3.6
DOE Sandia Nat. Lab.[a]	226,530	3.1
Rockwell Int.	197,405	2.7
Teledyne Inc.	181,145	2.5
Gencorp Inc.	175,455	2.4
SDI Institute	125,000	1.7
Textron	120,331	1.6
LTV Corp.	105,657	1.4
Flow General	90,226	1.2
Raytheon Co.	81,819	1.1
Martin Marietta	77,781	1.1
Total	$5,400,958	73.8

Note: Data are from FY 1983 to December 1986. Total contract values for this period equal $7,321 million. Since only three months of 1987 are included in the estimates, final figures may differ from those listed here.

a. Figures include $492 million in FY 1987 priced contract options that have yet to be exercised. Of this, Lockheed is to receive $34 million, Lawrence Livermore $83 million, EG&G $154 million, Los Alamos $123 million and Sandia $99 million.

Source: Council on Economic Priorities, *Star Wars: the Economic Fallout* (Cambridge, Ballinger, 1988) p. 51

have been distributed in contracts with firms, laboratories and universities. A study from the Council on Economic Priorities (CEP) in New York, has documented their distribution. Table 7.1 shows the 20 companies that received the largest SDI contracts in the period 1983–6, when the first $7 billion were spent. Together, they received $5.4 billion, three-quarters of total expenditure. Lockheed (with $720 million), General Motors (through its Hughes division, with $612 million), Boeing ($373 million), TRW ($373 million) and the Lawrence Livermore National Laboratories ($366 million) were the top five recipients.

Table 7.2: The Major US Military Firms

Company	Value of contracts ($ million)
General Dynamics	8,000
General Electric	6,800
McDonnell Douglas	6,600
Rockwell International	5,600
General Motors	5,100
Lockheed	4,900
Raytheon	4,100
Boeing	3,600
United Technologies	3,500
Grumman	3,000
Martin Marietta	2,900

Source: US Department of Defense, *100 companies receiving the largest dollar volume of prime contract awards, fiscal year 1986*, Washington DC, 1986.

Table 7.2 shows the US firms which in Fiscal Year 1986 received Defense Department contracts worth more than $2 billion. The overlap between the two lists is remarkable. In spite of the specific nature of space and electronics research envisaged for strategic defence, it is clear that traditional large US military firms leapt at the work. Among the first eight SDI corporate contractors for 1983–6 period are six of the Defense Department's top seven largest contractors and five of its top six contractors for RDT&E (Research, Development, Testing and Evaluation). These companies are increasingly dependent on military production. In 1985 well over half the sales of Lockheed, McDonnell Douglas, Rockwell and Martin Marietta were in military contracts, and in particular SDI now accounts for a sizeable share of total military contracts won by companies like Lockheed, General Motors-Hughes and Boeing.[7]

US universities are also increasingly involved in Star Wars research, clocking up a total of $200 million from SDI by 1986. The Massachusetts Institute of Technology, with its off-campus Lincoln Laboratory, received contracts for $60 million in 1985. In 1986, Utah State University received $8 million, the University of Texas $6 million, Georgia Tech $5.2 million, Johns Hopkins University $4.8 million, and Stanford $3.3 million.[8]

In fact, SDI research hardly represents a radical departure from the traditional style of development of new weapons systems by the major US military contractors. The same companies which built all US nuclear weapons have also been developing anti-missile work for years; it is then not surprising that various SDI projects, including those which are receiving the largest funds, are not new at all. As John Pike, of the Federation of American Scientists, has noted:

> Many of the projects in the SDI are not new weapons, but have in fact been under development for many years, although for applications other than missile defense. However, these systems were far too advanced for these other applications and had failed to receive approval for actual development. In a sense, SDI has become a technological orphanage. By incorporating these projects into Star Wars, with its formidable operational requirements, these systems have gained a new lease of life.[9]

While the outcome of these projects has often fallen short of the hopes raised by the Star Wars lobby's talk of 'futuristic' technologies, US military industry has not been let down by the profits accrued by Star Wars contractors. In 1984, the Defense Department's ten largest contractors had an average rate of return after taxes of 35 per cent – almost three times the 12.8 per cent average of US manufacturing industry as a whole.[10] As Senator William Proxmire pointed out, the major US military industries 'look at SDI as an insurance policy that will maintain their prosperity for the next two decades'.[11]

The US military industry's interest in promoting Star Wars can be seen in their intense lobbying of Congress, and in the extensive contributions from the military corporations' Political Action Committee

(PAC) to congressional candidates' election campaigns. The first 16 corporate contractors for SDI contributed close to $6 million to candidates running for federal office from 1983 to Spring 1986. Funds have been targeted to members of the Appropriations Subcommittees on Defense and the Armed Services Committees of the House and the Senate. In the period 1983–4, the 57 members of both House committees (13 per cent of all representatives) received 35 per cent of the $3.2 million paid. In the Senate, 36 members (slightly more than one-third of all senators) received 56 per cent of SDI PAC funds. In 1985–6, 30 per cent of the $2.4 million in PAC contributions went to 24 candidates: 17 of these were members of the two committees of the House and the Senate. While funds have been more or less evenly distributed between Republicans (56 per cent) and Democrats (44 per cent), an analysis of the voting record of the recipients of SDI PAC contributions showed significant support for high SDI funding.[12]

Additional evidence of the close network of Star Wars political and industrial interests is the geographical concentration of Star Wars research. 83 per cent of all SDI contracts between 1983 and 1986 have gone to five states: California ($3,255 million or 45 per cent of SDI expenditure), New Mexico ($1,230 million); Massachusetts ($718 million); Alabama ($535 million) and Washington ($403 million).[13]

If Star Wars is now a well-oiled political-industrial machine, where is it driving the US economy? It represents an increase of military spending in highly research- and capital-intensive areas. Estimates of the employment impact of SDI, according to the official Defense Economic Impact Modelling System, suggested that in 1986 SDI may have led to the creation of 66,000 jobs.[14] But SDI's focus on research and development means fewer jobs will be created for each million dollars spent, and with growing problems in financing public expenditure, SDI does not seem a particularly efficient way of expanding demand and employment in the US economy.

But developing SDI does demand substantial human and financial resources. Thousands of scientists and engineers have been driven to work on SDI, often leaving research in commercial fields. In 1986 their number was estimated at 5,700, with a further 3,200 technicians also involved.[15] As to the capital investment Star Wars requires, Robert Reich estimated in 1988 that SDI will control 'roughly 20 per cent of US high technology venture capital over the next four years'. He added:

> The problem is that never before on this scale have we entrusted so much technological development to the Pentagon in such a short time. A handful of Pentagon officials are pre-empting scientific

resources and picking winners and losers of the technology race, with large defense contractors advising them.[16]

In this perspective, SDI exemplifies the trend towards a military high-tech economy in the United States. While military research and development (R&D) already represents one-third of total US R&D expenditure (by far the highest share of advanced industrial countries excluding Britain) SDI is expected to account for 30 per cent of new military research, 10 per cent of all military R&D and possibly 5 per cent of the country's total private and public R&D expenditure.[17]

What will be the result of such an unprecedented concentration of innovative resources? SDI supporters have long claimed that Star Wars technologies – electronics, lasers, new materials – would lead to major innovations in all fields, with a significant impact on the whole economy. After six years of research, the evidence is still scanty.

According to Nathan Rosenberg, SDI 'represents a highly inefficient way of organising support for the civilian economy'. Secrecy and the specific military requirements of SDI raise major problems: 'the substantial divergence between the needs of the civilian economy and the military goal of strategic defense provides a formidable array of concerns which casts further doubt on the efficacy of SDI'.[18]

SDI and Industrial Technology Policy, edited by two Dutch analysts, concluded that 'from a standpoint of industrial technology policy *per se* SDI is not a cost effective approach and could be defined as counter productive'. The same doubts have been shared by Ann Markusen, who argued that 'there is little chance that the Strategic Defense Initiative will provide many commercial spinoffs', and by a British committee reviewing R&D policy: 'we remain unconvinced by the argument that the SDI will produce valuable civil spin-off'. Even a study by IBM on the first 350 SDI contracts in 1983–4 found that 'these contracts are not of any value to the civilian industry'.[19]

In the longer term, the decision to concentrate large resources in Star Wars may well have a lasting effect on the pace and direction of the US economy, particularly for industries exposed to international competition. The institutional structure, the military orientation and the specific applications envisaged in the programme raise serious doubts over the likelihood of such an effort producing generalised technological advances which could restore industry's productivity and competitiveness. In particular, it is hard to imagine how the Star Wars research projects could lead to a new generation of products and processes able to give US industry at least new powers to compete with the growing domination by Japanese and West European industry of commercial markets.

In the USA much of the pro-SDI argument still centres on the promise of the indirect industrial benefits of military research. But in Europe and Japan a new active policy has emerged in the 1980s. Here there are direct efforts to promote industrial innovation in a variety of well-funded high-technology programmes, developed by governments and large firms, which have targeted specific advances at the 'technological frontier'.[20]

The European and Japanese Response

Hopeless as it is on technological grounds, the USA may still score some political success with Star Wars. Under pressure from three sides – the military and political justifications of SDI as a defence programme; economic pressure arising from the amount of resources devoted to Star Wars; and the technological pressure of a concentrated R&D effort – Britain, West Germany, Israel, Italy and Japan have joined the Star Wars programme. But several countries, often with conservative governments, like the Netherlands, Denmark, Norway, Canada and Australia, have refused to participate in SDI research.

Many West European industries have looked for the much-promised SDI contracts. But very few have managed to overcome the strict protection of the US military 'market' and the highly restrictive conditions of the secret 'memorandum of understanding' signed between the USA and participating countries. The result is that of a total expenditure of between $12 billion and $14 billion by end-1987, only $100 million worth had gone in contracts to non-US firms. The total value of non-US contracts is expected to remain below $300 million by the end of 1990 – equivalent to 1 per cent of total SDI requested expenditure. It is not surprising that in 1987 a *Financial Times* survey of the British military industry found that more than half the firms originally interested in putting up long-term projects for SDI had stopped trying.[21]

By May 1988, Britain had received $61 million in contracts. Most of these went to the electronics firm Ferranti, and to the Ministry of Defence for a $10 million European 'architecture' study. This was mainly subcontracted to 18 private companies; $10 million were spent on laser research at a government laboratory. West Germany had received $48 million, mainly for research at Dornier and Messerschmitt-Bolkow-Blohm. Israel received contracts for $15 million. $7 million went to Italy and $3 million to France, which did not sign any official agreement with the US. Japan, which has agreed to join in SDI research, had not received one contract. The largest number of European firms has been involved in the seven contracts, worth $2 million each, assigned in December 1986 to consortia of different firms to study the architecture of a European strategic defence. The seven groups include 51 companies, 29 of which are European. The groups are headed by Messerschmitt-Bolkow-Blohm of Germany; Aerospatiale and Thomson of France; Italy's Snia BPD, a Fiat subsidiary; and four US companies: LTV, Science Applications International, RCA, and Lockheed with Hughes.[22]

In spite of West Europe's negligible share of Star Wars research, the USA's effort to involve its allies has succeeded to some extent in setting the agenda for the European debate on high technology and research policy. As resources for R&D and innovation are limited, Star Wars participation by European countries and firms means fewer openings to develop commercial technologies in other fields. Furthermore, accepting the terms set by the US for participation in SDI research – secrecy, control of results by the US Department of Defense, specific requirements and criteria for development – means some level of integration by European companies and institutions into the 'style' of US military technology. Once these rules are taken on board and this field is accepted as the ground for international competition, European industry can hardly hope to be more successful than its established US competitors. This is the kind of technological race that the US is certain to win.

Without entering into the European debate over participation in Star Wars research,[23] it is worth noting that since the European launch of Eureka as an alternative to SDI in civilian areas, the response from Europe has become weaker and more confused. There is now a general agreement among governments and companies that participation in Eureka is not 'incompatible' with work on SDI. In fact, the initial 'rivalry' between the two is giving way to some similarities in work on supercomputers, lasers, optics and new materials.

Japan's response to Star Wars has been a high-technology project of a different nature. The 'Human Frontier Science Programme' seems to have understood that SDI's fundamental challenge is to the direction of technological change, and it has suggested new areas and criteria for progress. These include human-environment relations, the problems of ageing, and biotechnologies. However, the Japanese programme is at a very early stage – as is Japanese participation in SDI – and it is too early to assess its scope and influence on the overall direction of Japanese high technology.[24]

US Power and the Contradictions of Star Wars

The use of Star Wars as a technological strategy has its economic and social base in forces in the United States which aim to preserve US international hegemony. In the post-war years, these encompassed a broad spectrum of US society, from multinational corporations and the 'military-industrial complex' to labour, with a domestic hegemony paralleling the one in the international arena. But the current attempt to revive US hegemony is opening up deep contradictions.

The US military economy, a major element of this strategy, is largely isolated from the world economy and international competition. The firms dominating military production are much less internationalised than those operating in commercial markets. In the 1980s the difference has increased further. Even in advanced technology sectors, US industrial production has become less competitive and US multinationals have increased production abroad, resulting in 1986 in the USA's first ever deficit of nearly $3 billion in the trade balance of high technology products.[25] At the same time, US military industries saw more rapid growth and became more domestically oriented, thanks to large defence contracts and to US technology policies focusing on military research.

But this contradiction between domestic growth and decline abroad is very much a US problem. All US firms, particularly multinational corporations, would benefit from renewed international leadership for the US, and a re-establishment of the post-war conditions that made possible the worldwide expansion of US capital. In the current crisis of US hegemony, these conditions may be established by other means – like a new international agreement between the advanced countries to coordinate management of the world economy, as some sectors of the neo-liberal establishment have proposed.

An international order where the US is no longer the undisputed leader leaves no major means to exert US power other than economic strength. Hence the growing discussion in the United States of the need to restructure the economy, to restore its competitiveness and ability to match other countries' performance. In this perspective, much neo-liberal thinking and debate within the Democratic Party is directly opposed to the technological strategy based on Star Wars – even though it may not question the USA's role as world leader and the need to maintain a large, if less exotic, military industry. Still, as hard choices on the budget and industrial policy will have to be made, a growing polarisation of interests could emerge between the domestic 'military-industrial complex' and the more internationalised sectors of the economy.

A second major contradiction can be found at the international level, in a growing confrontation with Western Europe and Japan. For Western Europe, the US strategy has meant technological and political subordination. Its success would lower Europe's capacity to innovate and pursue its own model of development. For Europe, this would mean following the US road towards an increasingly militarised economy and technology. One already visible consequence is that the powerful potential of new technologies is increasingly constrained by the political context – because they are locked into the existing power relations.

So far, the US strategy has been made possible only by continuing East–West confrontation, which has pushed Western Europe to support US policy and its technology-led arms race. In the new phase of detente, new opportunities to confront the US strategy and its contradictions may emerge for Western Europe, and new alternatives for Western relations may develop.

Alternatives for Western Relations

Western Europe has been divided in its response to the USA's technology strategy. Like the United States, the European position is characterised by a paradox. Europe's economy is by now too strong to let it fall behind the USA so that a new technology 'gap' emerges. But Western Europe is still too weak to challenge the USA's political leadership, and it is Japan that is emerging with the most powerful challenge to US economic and technological power.

The divisions and uncertainty within Europe have so far prevented the translation of its economic strength into political power, which would open up a new international order and a revision of the rules of trans-Atlantic relations. But the US strategy itself is highlighting the paradox of a Western Europe that keeps improving its economic performance, yet remains subordinate to US policies. A restructuring of Atlantic relations – both political and military – is inevitable, including a review of NATO and its strategy in today's new East–West context. The question is not whether this revision will happen, but *how*.

A wide set of economic relations are already being reorganised, ranging from exchange rates to financial flows, to trade rules. These have long been major areas of economic cooperation and conflict among states, and key tools for the regulation of the world economy. Now they have to be seen in combination with the longer-term international transformations in industry and technology, and with the new political and military dimension of Western relations.

In Europe, the pressure to play a more assertive international role is already evident, building on traditions of nationalism and aiming to combine West German economic strength with British and French military and nuclear forces. The road to Western Europe's emergence as a superpower is marked in economic terms by the unification by the end of 1992 of the domestic EC market. In military terms, it is laid out in the growing pressure for a new conventional arms race after the removal of Pershing 2 and Cruise missiles. However, such a strategy is weakened by the divisions between the European elites themselves, and it would be resisted by strong European political forces and opinion, not to mention the opposition of the USA and the USSR.

An opposite scenario could be drawn if East–West detente led Western Europe into a greater role as trade partner and provider of technology to the Eastern countries, should they move towards greater integration into the world economy. This would open up new opportunities for growth in long-stagnant European economies, and for a more autonomous role in international affairs, including in the key area of North–South relations. A phase of detente and cooperation in Europe could also bring about alternative security arrangements placing less emphasis on military force and more on political relations. Such a process would not mean a rupture of the Atlantic Alliance. It would mean a restructuring of Western relations, taking into account the changed positions of the USA and Europe and the diverging interests on either side of the Atlantic.

Moving away from military confrontation and towards greater autonomy in Europe, East and West, would also open the way for an end to Europe's division into two blocs. This would broaden the range of political alternatives in the West and make room for greater freedom and democracy in the East. It has been the perspective of an important part of Europe's peace movement in the 1980s, together with political forces, green movements and other voices. It is also a project for change that could parallel the growing vision of a 'Rainbow' coalition in the USA, which has so successfully challenged conventional wisdom about the USA's international role.

The technology strategy of Star Wars, with its industrial impact and international consequences, will do nothing to build a viable road to economic growth and technological progress. It cannot be described as a 'new frontier' for US growth, nor as a solution to the USA's current economic problems. As an economic policy of renewed 'military Keynesianism' as well as an industrial one, Star Wars looks like a failure. In the place of competitiveness and innovation in commercial fields, the Star Wars strategy puts military and political power at the centre of international relations. The principles of economic efficiency have been lost in the waste of an enormous military expenditure. The usefulness of technological progress is abandoned for the search for science-fiction space weapons.

The Reagan era is now over. The need is to reverse its priorities, both at home and internationally. Western economies could look for growth tailored to human needs, in civilian areas, with increasing control by civil society on economic and technological development. Meanwhile the international order could replace the instability, the strains and the arms race brought about by the USA's declining leadership with a more equal relationship between all countries.

8

Looking Southwards*

MARIANO AGUIRRE

'On NATO's Doorstep: Out-of-Area, Out-of-Mind', was the title on the front cover of the June 1988 issue of the magazine *NATO's Sixteen Nations*. But 'out-of-area' should not be out of mind anymore, for NATO's strategy is increasingly focusing on threats from outside its traditional area. After two Cold War periods between East and West, conflict scenarios are changing. Today the challenge comes from the South.

NATO and the Warsaw Pact were formed in 1949 and 1955 respectively. The military strategies and doctrines of the Western alliance have concentrated for most of its four decades on potential conflict in central Europe. But recently Western strategic analysts have redefined the possible conflict fronts. The North Atlantic Assembly declares, 'the Southern Region now constitutes not a flank, but a central front. It is one of the strategic centres of Europe.'[1] And the anticipated dangers are now wider in scope than the Soviet threat. They include terrorism, Islamic fundamentalism, attempts to blackmail the West by restricting its access to Third World resources, and rebellions against pro-Western governments.

In the two decades after the Second World War, Western Europe's principal preoccupation was Soviet and Eastern European aggression. At the same time, a process of decolonisation was taking place in the Third World. In most cases this meant that direct European domination was substituted by more modern and indirect US imperialism. While the United States expanded its military and economic hold over much of the globe, Western Europe seemed to withdraw to concentrate on post-war reconstruction and rebirth.

By the 1980s, Western Europe and Japan have reached a high level of development – which in many ways allows them to compete with the USA. In the military field, Western Europe has also gained great strength and an individual view on foreign politics and defence, although Western European states continue to depend strategically on the USA. They take a different view of the Soviet Union than the USA and as a result have a slightly different attitude in their foreign and

---

*Translated from the Spanish by Ellen Fichtner

defence policies. These differences within NATO are subtle and rarely tend to be made public, though in the last years some disagreements have seeped through the elegant walls of diplomacy. At his 1986 meeting with Mikhail Gorbachev in Reykjavik, former President Reagan discussed sweeping measures of nuclear disarmament. Western European leaders saw this as a sign of the impending withdrawal of the USA's security 'guarantees' to Europe, and some took the same view about the INF Treaty. Both the Reykjavik discussions and the Treaty drew some of these leaders into contradictory positions. On the one hand, they fear that the United States might retreat from its post-war commitment to defend Western Europe. On the other, they demand greater power within the decision-making process.

The ambiguous relationship between Western Europe and the United States also expresses itself in the Third World. The point is important because in future Western European leaders may have to make decisions related to intervention in the Third World which European public opinion will have to endorse or reject. In 1986, the then US Secretary of Defense Caspar Weinberger told the NATO allies: 'We must have leverage for action in corners of the globe far removed from the North Atlantic, places where developments can mightily affect NATO's security. We can only protect all of NATO and its flanks if we are fully prepared to take actions outside NATO theatres.'[2]

The 'Threat from the South'

Western Europe's post-war reconstruction and the process of decolonisation redefined its relationship with the Third World. Some European nations have partly maintained economic and/or strategic interests in former colonies: France, for instance, in Chad, Morocco and the Pacific Ocean. Others like Japan and West Germany (as well as Britain, France and Italy) have expanded their interests through corporations which invest extensively in countries like Brazil and Argentina. With some almost symbolic exceptions, for example Britain in Belize and the Falkland Islands, European Third World involvement since the end of the liberation struggles has been primarily economic.

Meanwhile, the United States consolidated its position as the premier hegemonic power through the influence of its banks, multinationals and armed forces. But after its defeat in Vietnam and following a wave of Third World revolutions, the US changed its view of Third World conflicts and of the role the European allies and Japan should play in them. Vietnam demonstrated to the United States that in a complex local war, deploying masses of troops and using military hardware indiscriminately were futile. At the same time, it generated strong public criticism in the USA and Europe. But even if in response to the 'Vietnam syndrome' US interventionism in the Third World declined for a while, the impact of rising oil prices, the fall of the Shah of Iran (a privileged ally according to the Nixon Doctrine) and the Soviet invasion of Afghanistan prompted a further reassessment of the US role in conflict in the Third World.

Fears that the security of the North could be endangered by threats and provocations from the South added a further aspect to this re-evaluation. Until Vietnam, the prevailing foreign policy doctrine had been the 'domino theory': if not stopped, communism in one Third World state would expand into neighbouring regions. But from 1979, what appeared to be in jeopardy was the security of the Western world – a term that was ambiguously defined. A sort of extended domino theory emerged: Reagan calculated the miles between Managua and Texas and deduced that Nicaragua's Sandinistas were a danger to Mexico, therefore to the United States. Hundreds of strategic studies surfaced, attempting to demonstrate that a Soviet advance towards Iran or Soviet control of the commercial shipping lanes near Cape Town could provoke the collapse of the Western economic system. The logic was this: the Soviet threat is intensified by its Third World allies. Add in the potential loss of access to valuable resources like petroleum, uranium, carbon and other minerals and the result is deep Western vulnerability. The perceived threat to Western interests in the Persian Gulf gave the United States an opportunity to reassert its stra-tegic and political leadership over other Western nations. This, the US strategists hoped, would in turn permit it to recover economic leader-ship.

Since the end of the 1970s, the United States has pressurised its allies to collaborate against these threats from the South, in 'out-of-area' operations. There are various reasons for this – to avoid the US being involved in Third World conflicts on its own, to reaffirm its leadership of NATO and to reassert its control in the Third World. 'The entire globe is now NATO's concern', stated Alexander Haig in 1980.[3] (Haig was the Supreme Allied Commander Europe from 1974 to 1979 and later became Reagan's first Secretary of State.) Pressure on Western Europe and Japan coincided with the development of the Rapid Deployment Force (RDF) which was later called the Central Command for Southwest Asia. It has more than 400,000 soldiers, backed by conventional and nuclear weapons of the US Navy and Air Force, and was ready to intervene in the Middle East and other areas of conflict. US ideologues were convinced that the chance of conflict on the central European front was becoming increasingly remote. In contrast, to deter potential threats from the South, Special Operations Forces were revitalised; new mobile divisions were created; modernised military transport was produced; and a 600-ship navy was planned.

The US desire to protect client governments in the Third World, maintain access to Third World natural resources and markets, plus Reagan's idea that the USA should shift to the offensive to roll back the supposed Soviet Third World successes of the 1970s, gave birth to a new strategy for conflict in the Third World. It is known as Low-Intensity Warfare.

Advance through the Flanks

Towards the end of the 1970s, a theory developed that the USSR was advancing its political influence by a series of manoeuvres on the 'flanks'. Early on in the Reagan administration this theory became the official line, and in 1986 the then Secretary of State George Shultz said:

> The ironic fact is, these new and elusive challenges have proliferated, in part, because of our success in deterring nuclear and conventional war. Our adversaries know they cannot prevail against us in either type of war: they turned to other methods. Low-intensity warfare is their answer to our conventional and nuclear strength – flanking maneuver, in military terms.[4]

To resist these challenges, the United States looked for support from its allies on international security policies. Although the allies later discussed 'out-of-area' contingencies in several regions, they initially focused on the Middle East. In the first place, the United States wanted to make use of Britain and France's colonial experience in that region. (Britain, for example, had kept a strong naval presence in the Persian Gulf until 1971 and sent a small patrol to the region again in the late 1970s.) Second, there were weak links in the allied force structure in central Europe, which made its flanks more vulnerable should the United States displace its troops to the Gulf.

The first time the 'out-of-area' programme was publicly presented to the allies was in the context of the Soviet invasion of Afghanistan. In January 1980, President Carter declared that the United States could not defend the Gulf alone and that it was necessary to coordinate 'our efforts with nations which are not located in the region but are heavily dependent, even more than we, on oil from that region'.[5] With the exception of Britain, the allies responded negatively to US requests to impose sanctions against Moscow and Kabul. Western European leaders were more concerned with maintaining detente with the Soviet bloc. They also saw different Soviet motives for invasion than those perceived by the Reagan administration. While Washington viewed Afghanistan as just another proof of Soviet expansionism, many European capitals saw it as a move which reflected internal conditions in Afghanistan. This difference of opinion was a primary factor impeding an expansion of 'out-of-area' operations.

None the less, the United States created its Rapid Deployment Force and during the Carter presidency planned to create a NATO force to act beyond the area of actual NATO responsibility. The Europeans were radically opposed to the idea. The first compromise solution came during the May 1980 meeting of the Defence Planning Committee where it was agreed to include a paragraph in the communique on the desirability of discussing 'out-of-area' forces.[6]

Out-of-area – an Old Problem

The alliance has debated 'out-of-area' operations almost since it was created. In December 1952 the North Atlantic Council recognised 'that resistance to direct or indirect aggression in any part of the world is an essential contribution to the common security of the free world'. At that time, France was fighting in South-east Asia and the Council's official statement expressed 'its wholehearted admiration for the valiant and long continued struggle by the French forces and the armies of the Associated States against the Communist aggression'.[7]

In December 1956, the alliance approved an influential report by the Italian Gaetano Martini, Norway's Halvard Lange and Canadian Lester Pearson on how to strengthen the cooperation of NATO countries. The report asserted:

NATO should not forget that the influence and the interest of its members are not confined to the area covered by the Treaty, and that common interests of the Atlantic Community can be seriously affected by developments outside the Treaty area. Therefore ... they should also be concerned with harmonising their policies in relation to other areas.[8]

When NATO was created, some European colonial powers hoped to leave open the possibility that the alliance would extend collective defence to its members' colonies. Only France was successful in this, in the case of Algeria. But when in 1958 Charles de Gaulle suggested creating a British-French-American directorate equipped to deal with Third World problems and to conduct possible 'out-of-area' operations, the US opposed this. In the 1950s and 1960s, while its multinationals and banks were expanding all over the globe, Washington wanted to consolidate the USA's image as a modern anti-colonial nation. Eisenhower's administration provided a good example of the US attitude in November 1956 when it refused to support the British-French-Israeli attempt to seize the Suez canal. The US decision on Suez also reflected its differences with Britain and France about the Middle East.[9]

The operation's failure discredited France and Britain and two months later made it easier for President Eisenhower to announce his Middle East Doctrine. He declared that the USA needed to fill the power vacuum left in the Middle East to prevent Soviet aggression. The Eisenhower doctrine was implemented in 1958 when the USA deployed 14,000 Marines to the Lebanon to block the extension of Egyptian leader Nasser's ideology.

The USA's projected 'anti-colonial' image changed in the 1960s, once Washington believed its influence had largely displaced France's and Britain's in some key regions. Until the mid-1960s the United States had used covert action to overthrow governments unfavourable to US interests and to replace them with allied regimes. The US had covertly intervened in Iran, Guatemala, Indonesia and British Guyana among other countries – it had only intervened militarily in the Dominican Republic and Vietnam. This policy defined the parameters of Washington's future interaction and relationship with its allies: the US government sought political and logistical support for its interventions, but it did not want direct allied participation in such operations.

During the Vietnam War, Washington received vital support from its allies. At the same time, an examination of the 'out-of-area' problem continued. An important shift came in May 1980 when the Defence Planning Committee affirmed for the first time that:

> The stability of the regions outside NATO boundaries, particularly in the Southwest Asia area, and the secure supply of essential commodities from this area are of crucial importance ... It is in the interests of members of the Alliance that countries which are in a position to do so should use their best efforts to help achieve peace and stability in Southwest Asia.

The statement recognised that the United States had assumed the role of defending that region and if US troops were to be sent to the Gulf, it could lead to an 'additional responsibility on all Allies for maintaining levels and standards of forces necessary for defence and deterrence in the NATO area'.[10]

In May 1981, the Defence Planning Committee made another important statement about 'out-of-area' activities. After the Soviet invasion of Afghanistan, the revolutions in Iran, Nicaragua and other countries, the failure of Carter's moderate policies, and the end of a decade of detente, it declared in a report that 'the policies which nations adopt outside the NATO area are a matter for national decision'. But it also noted that some situations beyond the NATO area could affect the security of its members. So NATO countries should prepare to consult each other and decide as quickly as possible the best way to respond to threats to their overall interests. For the first time there was mention of an 'out-of-area deployment of forces, in order to deter aggression and to respond to requests from other nations for help in resisting threats to their security or independence'. Equally, 'ministers also recognized that common objectives identified in such consultations may require members of the Alliance to facilitate out-of-area deployments in support of the vital interests of all'.[11]

The Allies provide Facilities
Since 1981, the North Atlantic Council has frequently declared that those allies capable of acting outside the NATO area should start preparing for such contingencies. All its statements insist on the non-alignment of Third World countries, the national character of any decision to act outside the NATO area, and the need for consultation to identify common objectives. At the same time, the possibility of broadening NATO responsibilities has not been excluded. In June 1982 the Council stated, 'Member countries of the Alliance, in a position to do so, are ready to help other sovereign nations to resist threats to their security and independence.'[12] At the same meeting, the problem of burden-sharing – the 'burden' being the cost to the USA of defending Western Europe – was linked to the issue of 'out-of-area' operations. In December 1982 a division of labour within the alliance was established. On the one hand are 'those countries such as the United States, which have the means to take action outside the Treaty area to deter threats to the vital interests of the West'. On the other hand are those which *would make an important contribution to the security of the Alliance by making available facilities to assist such deployments needed to strengthen deterrence in such areas*.[13] The same document indicated that the United States should consult the allies in the event of 'out-of-area' operations in defence of Western interests.

The war between Britain and Argentina in 1982 provides a good example of allied logistical support for 'out-of-area' operations. As an organisation, NATO was not actively involved in this war. But Western Europe offered support through the European Political Cooperation framework established by the European Community. In addition, the United States gave Britain assistance in the form of equipment, military intelligence and the use of bases.[14]

The Western military division of labour was further defined in June 1983. NATO foreign ministers declared that 'member nations, as they may decide, have a wide and diverse range of possibilities from which to choose in making useful contributions to promote stability and deterrence in regions outside the Treaty area'.[15] At the same time, the US government concluded that the best way for Western Europe to assist Washington's military activities in the Middle East was to build up its own military forces and increase the military potential in Europe.

A Multinational Force for Lebanon

While this debate was evolving within the alliance, things were happening on the international battlefield. In 1982, Britain, France, Italy and the US committed forces to create a Multinational Force (MNF) to intervene in the Lebanon conflict. Though each of these countries was theoretically separate and equal in this intervention, this was in fact not the case. For example, when France proposed deploying United Nations peace-keeping forces in Beirut, the United States vetoed the idea. The MNF was therefore acting outside the UN framework. The British and French governments argued that the MNF should maintain contact with all groups involved in the Lebanon conflict in order to achieve some form of consensus between the Amin Gemayel government and other factions. But Washington assumed leadership of the MNF, opting only to consult Israel and to implement a policy based primarily upon military intervention. Commenting on the operation, the Italian President Sandro Pertini declared that American forces in Lebanon were there 'to defend Israel and not peace'.[16]

A US Congressional Research Service report concluded:

> The MNF demonstrated an emerging tendency on the part of several NATO states to undertake greater responsibilities for their own security outside Europe. However, those same states believe that the U.S. policy governing its MNF contingent demonstrated poor judgement and an absence of a sense of measure in the utilization of military force. In part for these reasons, several important European allies believe that they can best protect certain critical interests by acting outside the umbrella of the US.[17]

Again in 1984, Italy, France and Britain collaborated with the United States, at the request of Egypt and Saudi Arabia, in clearing mines in the Red Sea which the Egyptian government claimed had been laid by Libya. But the Italian and French governments decided to act independently, bearing in mind the way the United States had behaved in Lebanon. They also refused to send representatives to the coordination committee established by the United States and Britain to supervise the movements of naval forces in the Red Sea.[18]

Another 'out-of-area' operation was the 1986 US attack on Libya. Since 1980 relations between the two countries had been extremely tense. In 1985 and 1986 the Reagan administration decided to initiate a potent public relations campaign to convince Americans and Europeans that the Libyan government was the main source of international terrorism. Although the US possessed data implicating Syria and Iran in terrorist attacks (especially in kidnappings of US citizens in the Middle East) it believed a media attack on either of these two countries would have had more dangerous consequences. Libya was an easier target; it was chosen to be the sacrificial lamb. Furthermore, focusing attention on Qaddafi was a way of hiding the secret hostages-for-arms deal that Washington had already made with the Khomeini government in Iran. And last but not least, the campaign against Libya was designed to assert US leadership over its European allies.[19]

In March and April 1986 the Reagan administration waged an active diplomatic and military campaign against Libya. Its principal argument was based on evidence it claimed to have that the Tripoli government was involved in the terrorist attack on *La Belle*, a Berlin discotheque frequently visited by US soldiers. The Western European response to the US initiative was mixed and ambiguous. Repaying US favours to Britain during the Falklands War, London allowed US bombers to fly from British bases. Indeed, Margaret Thatcher defended both the attack and Britain's collaboration. In contrast, France and Spain did not permit the aircraft to fly over their territory. But Felipe González's government did nothing to stop the USA using its bases in Spain to monitor aircraft on their way to their targets. In addition, 48 hours before the attack, tanker aircraft flew from the Spanish base in Zaragoza to Britain to accompany the F-111s and refuel them in-flight. The ships of the US Sixth Fleet returned to their Italian bases after fulfilling their part of the operation.

After the attack on Libya, the Italian and Spanish governments criticised the Reagan administration, though their criticism touched more on the method than the substance of US actions. In fact, almost all NATO governments agreed with the United States – even though evidence was lacking – that Libya exported terrorism. The allies imposed diplomatic and economic sanctions against Libya. In this manner, Washington received political and essential logistical support from Western Europe. Only two years later, it was made public that there was a fair possibility that the attack on the La Belle discotheque had been the work of services connected to the Syrian government.

Gulf Operations

The most spectacular 'out-of-area' operation took place in the Persian Gulf. On 17 May 1987, the Gulf War took on a new international dimension. The US frigate *Stark* was hit by a French-made Exocet missile launched by an Iraqi aircraft. The attack could have been a mistake. Or it might have been a ploy in Baghdad's long-term plan to involve conservative Arab countries and Western powers which opposed Iran in the conflict. If this was true, Iraq achieved its objective with a single missile directed at the right ship at the right moment. The US historian Theodore Draper commented that the attack on the *Stark* 'was heard in Washington as if it had come from an Iranian missile'.[20] Even though the White House had recently sold arms to Iran, the Reagan administration orchestrated news coverage of the incident so as to present Iran as the aggressor. The administration followed up by announcing its intention to protect the transport of oil in the Gulf from Iranian attack – even though, up to June 1987, Iraq had attacked 50 per cent more merchant ships than Iran in the 'tanker war' – and eleven Kuwaiti oil tankers were re-flagged as US ships.

Washington successfully campaigned for support for its Gulf intervention by stressing Western dependence on the region's vital resources. The US and five European NATO allies deployed a naval task force to guarantee the right of free passage through the Gulf.

At the peak of the operation, the US and its allies had 87 war ships in the Gulf. At different times, Washington stationed between 30 and 48 vessels there (some of them carrying nuclear weapons, though the Reagan administration would neither confirm nor deny this) with a force of 25,000 sailors. The daily cost of this operation was $1 million. It was the largest massing of US naval forces since the Vietnam War – but even so, most oil tankers went unescorted.[21]

By November 1987 France, Britain, Italy, Belgium and the Netherlands had around 39 ships in the region with 4,600 sailors. In addition, Japan – which is constitutionally prohibited from sending troops or vessels to other parts of the world – provided about $10 million to finance the Hyperfix mine detection system and had contributed $500 million in technical and financial assistance to states like Oman and Jordan.[22] West Germany deployed four vessels with 740 men to cover security in the Mediterranean. In May 1987, Spain succumbed to US pressure and offered to 'fill the gaps' created by the US Sixth Fleet's absence from the Mediterranean. Even Luxemburg, which has no navy, offered money for the Gulf operation.

On 18 November 1987, the *International Herald Tribune* reported that 'officially, allied governments continue to distance themselves from US actions' in the Gulf. The article went on to quote Anthony H. Cordesman, a specialist on the Gulf and former US defence official, who argued that NATO cooperation was 'optimal for the United States'. Furthermore, the article reported that 'several European officials cited the Gulf deployment as an initial exercise in the trans-Atlantic division of labor'. The device of common labour input politically coordinated through the Western European Union (WEU) would avoid problems: 'Loose coordination, rather than an integrated command that might offer greater military efficiency, eases political frictions among NATO alies when they confront threats to Western security outside the trans-Atlantic theater.'[23]

The European governments had insisted that their activity in the Persian Gulf should not be coordinated with that of the United States. Nevertheless, Bradford University's School of Peace Studies has argued in a study on British involvement in the Gulf that:

Close UK–US military cooperation already exists, extending to the establishment of jointly agreed rules of engagement in certain circumstances, backed up by a sharing of military tasks. In the event of a major escalation in the conflict extending to US forces it is difficult to see how British forces will avoid direct involvement.[24]

In July 1988 Iran and Iraq agreed on a ceasefire and the initiation of peace talks. In September, the United States stopped escorting US-flagged Kuwaiti tankers and some European forces left the Gulf. In early 1989 the tankers were returned to the Kuwaiti flag. This 'out-of-area' operation came to an end. The operation had a strong positive impact on both US and Western European public opinion, since governments presented the peace process as partly the result of deploying Western forces in the Gulf. An example of the 'peace through strength' theory, the tragedies of the *Stark* and the Iranian civil airliner destroyed by a US ship by mistake were treated as mere anecdotes. No serious thought was given to the potentially dangerous consequences that could easily have come from these events.

The Global Threat

NATO Europe has accepted a global conception of its security. The possibility of building a 'European Defense Pillar' coincides with a regeneration of the idea that Western Europe has its own interests in the Third World which should be defended. For the North Atlantic

Assembly the 'possible out-of-area challenges' to Western security interests 'are those where the military and/or economic security of alliance members or perhaps even the security of the Alliance itself could be threatened'.[25]

Proponents of the 'out-of-area' strategy identify an inordinate number of threats to Western security. For them the map of the world is covered with sensitive areas. There are the conflict zones, the countries under some degree of Soviet influence, and the regions which produce strategically important minerals and oil. There are also areas near important shipping lanes (both commercial and military), countries of particular strategic importance to the USA, and states which intend to use the UN Law of the Sea to extend their sovereignty beyond the three-mile limit of territorial waters. Particular attention is given to the areas producing the basic minerals for the defence industry like chromium, cobalt, manganese, tantalum and titanium, and to maintain the producing nations' economic dependency on NATO members.[26]

The list of vulnerable regions begins in the Middle East:

Contiguous to NATO's Southern Region; [it is a region] in a position to control all shipping in the Eastern Mediterranean; and serves as the crucial geostrategic link to the Gulf Region. Western economic interests in the Middle East are considerable and become vital in connection with the Gulf.[27]

Thus, strategic analysts argue, Arab oil producers could use the 'oil weapon' to obtain a Western position more favourable to the Palestinian cause.

The Horn of Africa (Ethiopia, Somalia, North Yemen, South Yemen) is the second sensitive area. The first three countries are located at the entrance of the Red Sea, placing them in a strategic position near the Persian Gulf. There is already a strong Western presence in this region through France and the USA, and plenty of potential exists for deploying additional forces.[28]

The third region where challenges might occur is in Southern Africa. The 'out-of-area' strategists face a serious political problem in South Africa. They condemn apartheid but they believe that human rights should be reconciled with Western security needs. The North Atlantic Assembly argues:

Without forgetting these principles and values for a minute, *other factors must be brought into view if a realistic policy is to be formed*: Western dependence on Southern Africa's strategic minerals, and the economic dependence of many African countries on the openly unjust South African system. Regional developments have profound implications for many Western interests, including security interests.[29]

Lamenting South Africa's predicament, *Navy International* declares, 'South Africa has been forced by the [UN] arms embargo to give up her erstwhile "Guardian of the Cape Sea Route" role'.[30]

Sub-Saharan Africa produces minerals vital for Western industry (manganese, vanadium, chromium, cobalt) and commerce (gold and diamonds). 'The heavy reliance of the United States and other industrial democracies on minerals imported from the region of Africa southward from Zaire is indisputed', affirms a study on strategic requirements for the US Army.[31] South Africa dominates the markets of chromium, manganese, vanadium and platinum which have a both a civilian and a military application. Supplies might be cut off or reduced as a result of several different contingencies: as a response by the apartheid state to an international boycott; as a form of blackmail by the Pretoria government against the West; as the result of a pro-Soviet faction taking power in South Africa (assuming Moscow also reverses its current policy of trying to foster trade between its allies in the Third World and Western nations); or as a consequence of civil war erupting in South Africa. The other fear concerning South Africa is that it has access to the South Atlantic commercial routes which carry raw materials from South America and Africa.

After the failed attempt to create a South Atlantic Treaty Organisation in the 1970s, Portuguese and Spanish naval forces are considering strengthening the NATO presence in that region. Because of the presumed South African weakness and the lack of a consistent NATO presence, this zone 'has thus effectively been allowed to become a major gap in the Western armour'.[32] The Soviet presence is seen through the relations Moscow maintains with Angola and the role of the Cuban military there. The theory that the African National Congress is a cover for a communist organisation is used to justify alarmism about a 'Soviet threat' in the area. But in fact Africa is not a priority in the USSR's foreign policy and Soviet influence in the region is restricted.

The Caribbean Basin, an abundant source of natural resources, is the fourth region where challenges to NATO security could arise. This area is a principal economic 'partner' for the United States. The big petroleum producers, Mexico and Venezuela, export much of their oil to the USA. Jamaica, Suriname and Guyana are important producers of bauxite. In addition, the Caribbean sea lanes and the Panama Canal are commercially important. In the event of a European conflict, the USA could send reinforcements to Europe from the Gulf of Mexico, while some divisions stationed on the US West coast would need to pass through the Panama Canal.

The threat to Central America and the Caribbean originates, according to proponents of 'out-of-area' operations, from the Cuban and Nicaraguan governments and the insurgents in El Salvador, Honduras and Guatemala. Cuba is considered a potential basing area for Soviet bombers, submarines and nuclear weapons. There are theories about the possible mobilisation of MIG 23 fighters from Cuba and Nicaragua, even though the latter has none of them. Some analysts believe that the 'aid and cooperation of the European allies in [US] policies are essential, if the credibility and effectiveness of the NATO alliance are to be maintained'.[33]

An Atlantic Council report in 1984 showed the Caribbean had grown in importance for the United States, because of the region's commercial and financial markets, petroleum production and refining operations, the flow of immigrants to the USA, and its accumulation of foreign debt. As a world power, the USA is forced to prove its global credibility. If it seems incapable of protecting its interests in the nearby Caribbean Basin, it risks an erosion of confidence in its promises to other areas.[34]

The same report suggested that the United States and other NATO governments with substantial interests in the Caribbean Basin could coordinate their policies and, in some cases, undertake joint actions. Assuming that all Western European nations are interested in the US capacity to supply the European continent in case of conflict, the report argues, they should offer military support.[35] Clearly, Washington has sought this cooperation despite its obvious disapproval of growing Western European economic presence in the area.

The last region considered a potential source of danger is North Africa. The Mediterranean is important both economically and militarily to alliance countries. The North Atlantic Council looks at this region in light of the following problems: Libya's support for international terrorism, good relations with the Soviet Union, and expansionist policies in Chad; social dissension in Tunisia, Algeria and Morocco; North Africa's population explosion, high unemployment, and consequent emigration to Europe; the impact of Islamic fundamentalism; the Western Sahara war where the Polisario Front, with the support of the Algerian government, is fighting against Morocco for national independence.[36]

Trans-Atlantic Tensions

Western European policy on the Middle East is eclectic. It is conditioned by past experience – historical links with the Arab World and the consequences of the widespread persecution of Jews in Europe which was capped by German genocide in the Second World War. Western European states recognise Israel's right to exist, but they seek a solution to the Israeli–Palestinian conflict – especially since the EC's Vienna Declaration in 1980. They also accept – with reservations at times – the right of the Palestine Liberation Organisation to participate in an international peace conference on the Middle East.

But for the United States, until a sudden change of policy in December 1988, the PLO was a terrorist group. US support for Israel is one of the strongest pillars of its Middle Eastern policy. For the United States, Israel is no less than an eastern extension of NATO. As the 'Iran–Contragate' affair revealed, Israel is more than an ordinary ally. It has become essential to Washington for covert action, arms trade and intelligence.

The direct confrontations between the Arab states and Israel have from time to time brought out the tensions between Washington and some European capitals. During the 1967 war, Charles de Gaulle criticised Israel strongly for annexing the West Bank of Jordan. The Arab-Israeli war of 1973 was a revealing experience for the Western Europeans: the United States actively took sides with Israel and used Portuguese and West German bases – in the first case with authorisation from the government, in the second, secretly – to supply the Israeli army. The USA also declared a worldwide military alert without consulting other NATO members. Former Secretary of State Henry Kissinger wrote years later that with a problem like Israel, the US was not willing to accept 'a judgment different from our own'. He explained, 'Allies should be consulted whenever possible. But emergencies are sure to arise again; and it will not be in anyone's interest if the chief protector of free world security is hamstrung by bureaucratic procedure.'[37] Faced with Washington's unilateral action and strong pro-Israeli attitude, and with differences over oil and energy conservation, the European allies began to develop their own policy on the Middle East.

Western European states were especially worried about US military actions in the Middle East and tried to keep their distance so that they could be dissociated from any possible troop mobilisation by Washington. The Europeans continue to bear in mind the Korean and Vietnam Wars, which make them cautious about the 'rules of engagement' in case limited military engagement leads to a more serious conflict.[38] Even an extremely pro-US government like Margaret Thatcher's carefully pointed out the limitations of its naval participation in the Persian Gulf. In July 1984, Foreign Minister Geoffrey Howe explained to the Soviet Foreign Minister Andrei Gromyko that if Britain deployed naval forces in the Gulf, it would do so in order to guarantee the right of free navigation and not go beyond that.[39]

Another important trans-Atlantic difference concerns the interpretation of Soviet policy. Analysts – whether US or European – who favour strong US leadership and an activist policy stress the Soviet danger, and tend to exaggerate the USSR's capabilities and influence in the Third World. Those who are more positive about detente assess Moscow's influence more carefully. They think the Soviet Union actually plans to diminish its commitments in the Third World. The USA's *linkage* theory, which makes good East–West relations conditional on 'good conduct' by the USSR, has caused problems for Europeans. It has also been argued that the less-developed economic nations are not as keen to form close economic relations with the USSR today than they were. And despite an increase in naval forces over the last few years, the Soviet offensive capability is limited.[40] Prior to the Gorbachev era, a report by the North Atlantic Assembly declared:

> While recognizing the Soviet penchant to use its power and influence to exacerbate local differences, the Soviet Union is not, in fact, considered the most serious threat to regional stability in South-West Asia. It was repeatedly emphasized (by the consulted sources of the Rapporteur), in fact, that a Soviet invasion was not considered probable. The major regional problems are thought to be political and economic in nature, rather than military.[41]

Some US analysts view the US as a superpower with global interests, while the European allies have only regional concerns. Former US Under-Secretary of State Lawrence Eagleburger (now Deputy Secretary of State in the Bush administration) wrote that Western Europeans have a hard time understanding 'the difficult requirements for a nation with global responsibilities (as opposed to those) with more regional concerns'.[42] Another more sophisticated viewpoint does not criticise the European allies for such failings, but proposes a more effective international division of military labour.

The Burden-sharing Debate

It is not easy for Western European states to intervene actively in the Third World. In the first place, economic conditions do not allow them to raise their military spending substantially. Some countries, like West Germany, also have demographic problems limiting the number of citizens who can be brought into the armed forces. And though public opinion is steadily becoming politically more conservative, there is still reluctance to involve NATO militarily in the Third World.

The United States maintains that while it invests heavily in the defence of Western Europe, European NATO members resist collaborating with it even to protect oil supplies, despite the fact that oil is fundamental to Europe's industrial and economic performance. The US government contrasts its expenditure of 6.9 per cent of Gross National Product on the military with the proportion spent by Western European states: the Federal Republic of Germany spends 3.1 per cent; Italy 2.7 per cent; and except for Britain, which spends about 5 per cent, the rest of Western Europe devotes less than 4 per cent of GNP to the military.

The US argument is that the European allies are taking a free ride, refusing to share the burden of their defence fairly, and using the money not spent on defence to subsidise their exports – which have helped create the huge US trade deficit. Similar complaints are made about Japan. This debate on burden-sharing is linked to the 'out-of-area' issue, for the argument goes on to state that the US spends heavily to defend the Persian Gulf oil routes, even though it is less dependent on oil from that region than are Japan and Western Europe.[43]

This type of argument ignores several important factors. Trans-Atlantic trade disputes in this decade have originated primarily from high US interest rates designed to attract European capital and from protectionist measures introduced by the USA itself. Fundamentally, however, the burden-sharing argument ignores the fact that the United States is a world power, but Western European states are not. Most US military spending is absorbed by its international role, of which Western European deployments are only one large part. The argument is based on false comparisons.

The huge Federal budget deficit forced the Reagan administration to reduce its military spending plans. Cutting US forces in Europe in the 1990s has become a realistic possibility. But first the USA will want to ensure that its allies will not opt for denuclearisation. It will want to protect its economic interests and political influence. It will also try to ensure that Western European states fill any 'gaps' left by departing US forces.

The debate about burden-sharing has prompted the Eurogroup – made up of European NATO states except France – to outline the different ways in which it contributes actively to collective defence.

The group's aim was to point out the existing equilibrium between the two sides of the Atlantic. Among other things, the Europeans have stressed their role in 'security outside the NATO area'. A Eurogroup pamphlet, referring to the common interests of the allies beyond the NATO area, details European forces which are permanently deployed in Africa, the Indian Ocean, the Far East and Central America. It notes that more than 1,000 Europeans serve as training and consulting personnel in countries outside the NATO area.[44]

Compensate, Facilitate, Participate

Despite the differences, some Western European countries have adopted measures supporting US 'out-of-area' policy. In 1980, 1981 and 1982, the forces of eight NATO members participated with the US in troop manoeuvres. The FRG granted overflight rights, en-route access and support for deploying US forces. The 1981–6 NATO Force Goals and Long Term Defense Program developed new projects on equipment, readiness, reinforcement, reserve mobilisation, war reserve stocks, maritime measures, air defence and communications – all designed to reinforce European defence in case the United States should send forces to the Persian Gulf. Ten NATO members committed themselves to providing NATO with about 100 civilian vessels to transport forces from the United States should conflicts develop simultaneously in the Gulf and Europe. Nine promised freight and passenger aircraft for the same role.[45] In April 1982, Bonn and Washington signed a support agreement in which the FRG pledged 90,000 soldiers to fulfil the duties of European-based US troops who in a war would have to be removed for contingencies elsewhere.

All these measures can be summarised in the formula: *compensation, facilitation and participation*. 'Compensation' means filling gaps if US troops are withdrawn from Europe for other tasks. 'Facilitation' signifies that US forces, en route to the Persian Gulf or elsewhere, may fly over European countries and make use of bases and installations there. And finally, 'participation' means involving European forces directly in Third World actions. This formula is normally qualified by adding that it is *ad hoc*, which means that there is no need for a joint decision-making process, but that each 'out-of-area' case should be studied and decided upon by the country or countries which believe their interests are at risk.[46]

If NATO proves an inadequate forum for coordinating 'out-of-area' actions, other more appropriate solutions are sought. One is the Western European Union (WEU). It remained inactive for almost 30 years after its creation in 1954. But then, motivated by the idea of creating a 'European pillar' within NATO, François Mitterrand's government decided to promote the organisation: in 1984, it proposed creating a European army, something that could act beyond NATO boundaries and which would be based on a revitalised WEU.

The President of the WEU Assembly, Charles Goerens, has explained that since 1985 one of the major WEU functions was 'favouring the activities [of the Europeans] outside the area that is covered by NATO – principally, within the Persian Gulf'.[47] President Reagan's former special assistant for national security affairs, Geoffrey Kemp, stated that in facing conflicts in Central America or the Philippines a European military contribution could not be expected, but that in the case of the Middle East or Europe itself, 'The USA should encourage them to work within the revitalized Western European Union to establish a parallel set of European defense ventures within the NATO framework.'[48]

The decision to send European warships and minesweepers to the Persian Gulf was taken at a meeting of the WEU in London in September 1987. Shortly before the decision was made, a British newspaper said with brutal frankness:

> Its [the WEU's] main purpose is to enable the Europeans to speak to Washington, their main partner, with one voice. A secondary function is to allow some governments [not Britain] to take decisions which would be unpopular if made in response to a request from Washington but are acceptable in a European context.[49]

Likewise, it has been suggested that one reason why Spain recently joined the WEU is so that it can contribute to a rapid action force.

The Threat from the Mediterranean

While examining the challenges on the Southern flank, strategists have re-evaluated the Mediterranean area. Their opinion is that it contains so many threats that the alliance does not have sufficient means to deal with them.

The Southern flank has turned into the *real* Central Front. In November 1983 the North Atlantic Assembly expressed the following judgement: 'The Alliance has been dominated in the past by concerns of the Central Region. It is time to devote more attention and funds to the Southern Region.'[50] And the Chief of Staff, Headquarters Allied Forces Southern Europe, wrote:

> The vital resources that lie just beyond NATO's border to the South and East, taken in conjunction with the diversity and number of

non-traditional threats, leads me to the judgment that the center of NATO's strategic concern has shifted towards the Southern Region. Although we lack the capability to do much about them by ourselves, we in the Southern Region are in the forefront of these new challenges ...[51]

Confronted with these multiple threats, the United States and Western Europe are developing parallel theories. While US analysts focus more on the Soviet danger, Europeans are worried about developments like Islamic unity. But both agree that, whether the problem is an indirect Moscow strategy or a direct strategy in the less-developed countries, the danger comes from the Third World.[52]

The French 'new right' almost always includes in its books an attack against the Third World and its European allies. The totalitarian theory of the Cold War has been combined with the one about the Soviet flank advance, using Cuba, Nicaragua, Vietnam, Angola or Algeria as examples. Likewise, the right sees the United Nations and all its agencies (and in particular UNESCO) as bodies serving Moscow's objectives in promoting dictatorial Third World systems: attacking the free market; advocating communist, socialist and pacifist ideologies; and imposing limits on the free West through legislation like the Law of the Sea.[53]

Everything 'has turned global, diffuse and multiform', declare French authors Claude Nigoul and Maurice Torrelli in a work published by the Fondation pour les Etudes de Défense Nationale.[54] Nigoul and Torrelli argue that population growth in North Africa, Islamic expansionism, neutralism and the movement to make the Mediterranean a nuclear-free zone are aggressive factors which could harm Mediterranean stability. Their book exemplifies European Atlanticist strategic analysis and anti-Third World attitudes, combined with the anti-pacifism prevalent in France. With veiled racist overtones, the authors worry about immigration from the Third World to the North and the similarity between anti-imperialism and Islamic fundamentalism.[55]

While the authors admit that, in strategic terms, Western Europe today is not very vulnerable to threats to its supplies of oil and other essential raw materials, they believe Europe is threatened by an indirect strategy. Libya, aided by international terrorism, is the principal actor in this theory. They also argue that a strategy of 'regional neutralisation and exclusion of the Western world' exists in the Mediterranean, in which the neutral island of Malta plays the main role. According to this analysis, a 'red chain' extends from Albania through Malta to Libya. From there it could extend to the African countries that have relations with Moscow: Burkina Faso, Benin, the Congo and Angola. The 'red chain' helps the Soviets preserve their 'security space' and control the natural resources of Sub-Saharan Africa. The authors further argue that this neutralisation strategy promotes nuclear-free zones in the Middle East and the Balkans and the creation of a peace zone in the Mediterranean. Criticising 'the mobilisation myth of disarmament', they declare that the UN and the Conference on Security and Cooperation in Europe accept initiatives promoted by the Soviet Union, Eastern Europe, Malta and the non-aligned countries. All of this they see as directed towards Moscow's objective: a nuclear-free and neutral Europe.[56]

Washington – the Unifying Axis

A complementary analysis of the Mediterranean sees it as a vital link with the Persian Gulf. Thus it has been transformed into one of the world's most important strategic areas. US Admiral Harry Train states:

> The key word in Mediterranean strategic planning is 'join'. For, rather than presenting a barrier, the Mediterranean 'joins'. It joins Middle East oil with Western Europe. It joins Indian Ocean shipping with the Atlantic Ocean. It joins Soviet ice-free Black Sea ports with the Atlantic and Indian Ocean trade routes. It joins together the Southern NATO partners. And it joins some of the West's most important industrial nations with their markets and resources.[57]

Given the Mediterranean's importance, the United States views itself as the fundamental axis to confront threats to the area. European Atlanticist opinion accepts this assessment.[58] This allows Washington to fit NATO's *regional* strategy into its own *global* approach.

The new importance of the Mediterranean in overall US strategy brings out the relationship between 'out-of-area' operations and the US Navy's maritime strategy adopted during the Reagan era. In accord with the global and unifying conception of security, this maritime strategy aims to integrate allied navies further into US operations.[59] Accordingly the Mediterranean NATO states are building up their naval air forces and equipping themselves for rapid intervention operations. Numerical increases and qualitative improvements carry this policy forward in France, Italy, Spain and Portugal. The result is a proliferation of fighter planes, submarines, frigates, lightly equipped missile units and the construction of aircraft carriers like the *Príncipe de Asturias* and the *Garibaldi* in Spain and Italy.[60] The Spanish case exemplifies this policy: in negotiations about its duties in NATO, the emphasis is on maritime air operations for the control of the Straits of Gibraltar, the western Mediterranean and the eastern Atlantic Ocean as far west as the Canary Islands.

In the 1980s, France, Italy and Spain created rapid action forces. Soon Portugal, Greece and Turkey could have similar forces. Although French rapid action forces are designed for use on the Central Front, the government does not reject the idea that they could be used for 'out-of-area' operations. In the Italian case, despite speculation about their use as a peace-keeping force, Italian strategic analysts strongly deny that there is a willingness to deploy them 'out of area'.

Military sources consulted for this investigation believe that Spanish and Italian rapid action forces are connected with the revitalisation of the Allied Mobile Forces (AMF). Created by six NATO countries in 1961, the AMF has the somewhat symbolic mission of demonstrating allied solidarity by being ready to act jointly to resist enemy attacks. Analysts now believe that rapid intervention forces could complement the AMF once it is reformed to make it more effective.[61]

The importance of the Southern Flank means US bases are being considered as possible support points for the Rapid Deployment Force. In a study of the US Army's strategic requirements to the year 2000, Spain, for example, is cited as an area where some divisions making up the RDF could be stationed. The study concludes that Spain has 'adequate training areas' and is an appropriate country from which to send forces to Latin America and North Africa.[62] A Portuguese expert, Alvaro Vasconcelos, stated that the US RDF 'can draw great advantages from facilities in Portugal, Spain and Morocco'. Even though the Spanish government denies it, Vasconcelos states that for this reason 'the United States has obtained facilities in Zaragoza, Morón, Torrejón and Rota [all in Spain], and in the aeronaval base of Kenitra in Morocco'.[63]

There is, however, a consensus among European and US analysts that governments which host US bases will react cautiously when the US asks them to let these be used for 'out-of-area' activities.[64] The formula adopted by the Mediterranean NATO states seems to consist of not supporting 'out-of-area' operations actively, but of allowing the United States to maintain and modernise any necessary infrastructure to carry out such activities. An example is Portugal.

In 1967, the bases on the Portuguese Azores islands were readily made available to help in the US effort to assist Israel during its war with the Arab states. Today, the Portuguese government is not so compliant.

In 1984 it became known that Washington wanted to use the Lajes base in the Azores for the Rapid Deployment Force. In 1987, it was reported that the Azores facilities were being modernised to strengthen capabilities for Atlantic anti-submarine warfare and 'out-of-area' operations. In particular, the Azores were reportedly used as a base for naval exercises reaching as far south as Angola.[65] In effect, NATO's regional command had established a plan covering operations far south of the Tropic of Cancer, which is the limit of the NATO area. Rear Admiral Hamm, Deputy Commander-in-Chief of the Iberian Atlantic Area, said it was a contingency plan to protect the supply routes for oil and bauxite, made necessary because the USSR had ships and aircraft in Angola.[66]

But Portugal's willingness to allow the Azores bases to be used for 'out-of-area' operations had changed. An agreement governing the bases was signed on 18 May 1984, replacing a 1951 accord. New conditions specified that the Portuguese would provide the US with use of the facilities 'within the framework of the North Atlantic Treaty'. Almost all political analysts believe the change in the terms of agreement reflected Portugal's discontent about the level of US military aid it received. If they are right, the position could change if aid were more generous. But there are also other more complex political factors. Between the freedom of action enjoyed by the US military in 1967 and the restrictions placed on it in the 1980s came the Portuguese revolution of April 1975 and a democratic political system in Portugal. Today Portuguese public opinion resists subordinating national interests to US foreign policy, and it has the capacity to express itself.

The same formula of helping the USA by providing infrastructure while renegotiating agreement on US bases was applied by Felipe González's government in Spain. On the one hand, the Spanish government managed to get Washington to withdraw 72 US F-16 aircraft from its base in Torrejón de Ardoz, near Madrid. Instead these will be stationed in Italy. On the other, the US base in Rota remains, and has been recently modernised for 'out-of-area' operations, control of the Mediterranean and sending forces towards North Africa and the Middle East. Rota was not even included in the negotiating process. Both sides took it for granted that Rota would continue under US control.

Tendencies and Ambiguities

The conditions for expanding the formal limits of the Atlantic Alliance do not exist at present, but the trend of recent years is troublesome. The evolving situation is defined by several features, not least a consensus among allied governments over the necessity of acting outside the NATO area, and by the reaffirmation of the United States as the leading power in much of the Third World. It has been accepted that 'out-of-area' operations cannot be coordinated by NATO; instead organisations like the WEU may carry out the task. Western European governments have also accepted that they will have to compensate for any shortfalls in US forces, which implies a probable increase in their military budgets. The situation of NATO's Southern Flank countries is ambiguous: governments' unwillingness to collaborate openly in 'out-of-area' operations is balanced by their readiness to grant Washington the right to maintain and modernise facilities and bases which are needed to make such operations feasible. Finally, racism, the growth of the 'new right' and anti-Third World sentiment in Western Europe predispose its public to accept interventionism in the Third World. While the danger of NATO forces intervening in the Third World should not be exaggerated, one should not discount the possibility that some European nations may undertake unilateral initiatives or participate in US military adventures.

The alliance has rules of negotiation and maybe Washington is asking for a lot from its allies: bases, facilities, flight permits, political support and European willingness to increase forces on the Southern Flank. In October 1987, the US Congressional Committee on Military Appropriations expressed concern about 'the failure of US NATO allies to provide adequate support for alliance security interests outside the NATO region. Currently, there is no formal organization within the NATO structure for developing and coordinating NATO policies outside the prescribed treaty area.'[67] But in January 1988, the Reagan administration was pleased with allied cooperation and coordination when Britain, France and Italy helped with US mine-sweeping in the Gulf. It was also relieved, as it could then justify to Congress the $1 million daily cost of the operation.[68] Washington did not formally participate in that coordination; instead the US was seeking a division of labour within the alliance rather than filling the old leadership role. Modern war is not only decided by weapons. A wide and sophisticated infrastructure has also become necessary. The Europeans will probably not fire any missiles nor land in any distant country, but they may well act as the indispensable rearguard and their political responsibility will be concomitant to this task.

In 1980 the then Chancellor of West Germany, Helmut Schmidt, called for an explicit military division of labour in the alliance:

The truth is: number one, we cannot send troops into the Persian Gulf. We have constitutional inhibitions. Number two, we have no inhibitions on seeing American troops being moved from Europe to the Persian Gulf. On the contrary ... there should be a division of labour in the Western defence alliance.[69]

The foreign policy of the United States towards the regions it considers strategically important is mainly based on the issues of arms exports, the promotion of a supposed military balance and the possibility of direct or indirect military intervention. Western Europe has followed the US lead on arms diplomacy, particularly in the Middle East, and its disastrous results can be seen in the Iran-Iraq war. Formally, all Western governments wanted peace between Tehran and Baghdad, but there was also a secret policy. Its aim was both to prevent Iran winning – as that could lead to an expansion of Islamic fundamentalism – and to impede an Iraqi victory for fear that it would leave Iraq with too much power in the region. Consequently, the USA, France and other Western European governments, as well as the USSR, all sold arms to both sides.[70]

Rethinking Security

The path Western Europe is taking with the 'out-of-area' strategy is dangerous and should be rethought. It is in any case likely to be resisted by strong segments of domestic political opinion in each country. But public resistance will fail to reach its full potential if it focuses only on objecting to each specific 'out-of-area' contingency as it arises. What is needed alongside that resistance, plus pressure on the USA against its interventionism, is a completely new approach to the basic issue of security.

Numerous studies of the present decade have sought to redefine the concept of security. They have expanded it beyond its military aspect – defending a nation's citizens against attack. Now ecological and environmental issues come into the idea of security. The studies have asked how we can guarantee access to the minimal level of resources required for a reasonable degree of prosperity.

To make this possible, new norms of global security based on understanding the concept of interdependence must be established. These are needed because although all nations have needs, not every country has the same economic potential, level of development or natural resources. The issue is far from simple, but dealing with it by exclusively military means can only lead to a situation in which the strongest states monopolise power and weaker ones resist by such means as terrorism.[71] Military solutions to resource problems – like the rapid occupation of oil fields – produce results which are exciting only in war-games and military manuals.[72]

A concept of interdependent global security may begin by establishing agreements designed to strike a balance between the different requirements of countries which produce raw materials and those which consume them. Any such agreements must balance the need to conserve natural resources with the producing countries' need to continue to export.

Western Europe should help countries which export raw materials to diversify their economies, so that they are no longer financially dependent on one primary export. To broaden their economic base, these countries need technology, knowledge, capital goods, and cooperation from the industrialised world. Advanced industrial states which seek to assist the development of countries with natural resources could reach mutually beneficial agreements with them. The next step would be to implement agreements on aid and development for other countries which lack resources – nations such as Ethiopia and Haiti – for they are threatened with starvation on the sidelines of the international economy.

Both producers and importers of primary goods must look for alternative energy sources and replacement materials. Relying on nuclear energy is very risky, as Chernobyl has proved. And current nuclear technology is far more expensive than was claimed a few decades ago. Natural gas and coal could substitute for petroleum in many areas. In addition, non-conventional energy sources should be explored further: for example, biomass, solar and geo-thermal energy; biogas; hydrogen-based energy systems; wind, wave and tidal energy; and crops especially designed to produce combustibles.[73] None of these sources alone would be likely even partly to solve the problem of dependence on oil. But taken together with energy conservation, they could constitute a realistic alternative. These steps would not only limit external resource dependency, but also aid in the expansion of a global security policy based on the idea of resource conservation.[74]

Nuclear Umbrellas, Political Dependencies

Western Europe is trapped by its strategic dependence on the United States. If it decides not to give in to US pressures to assist in operations in Third World countries, it is faced with the possibility of Washington withdrawing troops from Europe. This constitutes the most effective pressure the United States could exert on its allies, since it plays directly on the ambiguity of the Euro-American relationship. Charles Kupchan makes this point in his discussion of European deployment of Cruise and Pershing missiles:

The Europeans were concerned about influencing not only the

content of U.S. policy, but also its general orientation. One of the principal reasons behind NATO's decision to deploy American inter-mediate-range missiles had been to prevent the 'decoupling' of the United States from Europe in the event of a Soviet attack through the central front. In a similar sense, the Europeans feared that America's interests outside NATO's boundaries – specifically in the Middle East and East Asia – might decouple the United States from its close ties with Europe. If the Europeans did not show at least some support for America's effort outside the area, then the strength of America's military commitment to Europe could well be dimin-ished.[75]

The short name for this process is blackmail. It is largely an implied warning; the fear of US military reductions is so deeply embedded in Western Europe's political and military establishment that Wash-ington barely needs to utter the threat out loud.

An important step in establishing a new security policy is in the field of arms control. Progress here could weaken the effect of this veiled blackmail. The new detente makes possible treaties on reducing conventional and nuclear forces in Europe which should further improve East–West relations. It could also make an eventual with-drawal of US forces less alarming. Going one step further, if the importance of NATO and the Warsaw Pact were to decline, Western European governments would be better able to resist US pressure to participate in Third World military actions.

At the same time, the idea of 'strengthening the European pillar in NATO' holds its own dangers. It could lead to a new military bloc in which French and British nuclear forces replace those of the USA. If this were to happen, both Europe and the Third World would be at risk. For Europe, it could lead to a new round of confrontation and higher military spending. For the Third World, it would pose a new threat to independence. Third World countries often want greater Western European involvement to moderate the USA's interven-tionism; but if Western Europe starts operating as a new bloc, the result could be a military temptation to exert greater power over less-developed countries.

Western European countries must resist the temptation to create a new imperialist role for themselves. Instead they should seek to strengthen and reform the United Nations to make it less dependent on the opinions of the superpowers concerning the resolution of conflicts. Parallel to this, they must prepare their military forces to play an active role in UN peace-keeping operations. For in the long run the real protection of European interests will not be based on rapid action forces and 'out-of-area' operations. It will be found through detente, common security, development in the Third World, environmental protection, the search for alternative energy sources, the promotion of democracy and the preservation of national sovereignty.

Notes and References

All congressional hearings and official US documents referred to were published by the US Government Printing Office in the calendar year before the fiscal year (FY).

1 The Changing Strategic Context

1. See the reports of the Alternative Defence Commission – *Defence Without the Bomb* (London: Taylor & Francis, 1983); *Without the Bomb* (London: Paladin, 1985); and *The Politics of Alternative Defence* (London: Paladin, 1987) – and of the Palme Commission on Disarmament and Security Issues – *Common Security* (London: Pan Books, 1982).
2. E.P. Thompson might be taken to exemplify the first school – see 'Beyond the Cold War' in *Zero Option* (London: Merlin Press, 1982) – and Fred Halliday the second – *The Making of the Second Cold War* (London: Verso, 1983).
3. Shifts in Soviet thinking are explored in Stephen Shenfield, *The Nuclear Predicament* (London: Routledge & Kegan Paul, 1987).
4. Thompson's polemic was first published as a pamphlet – *Protest and Survive* (London: CND, 1980) – and revised to form the opening essay in Thompson and Dan Smith, eds, *Protest and Survive* (Harmondsworth: Penguin, 1980). Howard's reply was 'Surviving a Protest', *Encounter*, Vol LV, No 5, Nov 1980.
5. Michael Howard, 'The Gorbachev Challenge and the Defence of the West', *Survival*, Vol XXX, No 6, Nov/Dec 1988.
6. Extracts printed in *Guardian*, 8 Dec 1988.
7. Quoted in *Guardian*, 3 Mar 1987.
8. Quoted by Jamie Dettmer, 'Geneva Talks Reach Stalemate', *END Journal*, Summer 1986.
9. Alain C. Enthoven and K. Wayne Smith, *How Much Is Enough? Shaping the Defense Program 1961–1969* (New York: Harper & Row, 1971) pp. 132–42.
10. 'Study Insists NATO Can Defend Itself', *Washington Post*, 7 June 1973.
11. 'Pentagon Study Finds NATO's Conventional Forces Can Deter Attack', *International Herald Tribune*, 1 Dec 1987.
12. Mark Urban and Peter Pringle, 'Assessing the Arms Divide', *Independent*, 7 May 1987.

13. For fuller descriptions of these events, see my *Pressure: How America Runs NATO* (London: Bloomsbury, 1989) Chapter 5.
14. Paul Kennedy, *The Rise and Fall of the Great Powers* (New York: Random House, 1987).
15. Lt Col J.D. Waghelstein, 'Post-Vietnam Counterinsurgency Warfare', *Military Review*, May 1985.
16. Commission on Integrated Long-Term Strategy, *Discriminate Deterrence* (Washington DC: US Government Printing Office, Jan 1988).
17. *Western Defence: The European Role in NATO* (Brussels: Eurogroup, May 1988).
18. Harold Brown, *Department of Defense Annual Report Fiscal Year 1982* (Washington DC: US DoD, 1981) p. 63.
19. Quoted in *Observer*, 15 June 1986.

2 Bush and NATO – Comes the Reformation

1. Notre Dame University Address, South Bend, Indiana, 1 Nov 1988 – text provided by campaign.
2. San Francisco speech, quoted in David Broder, 'Bush and the Fateful First Few Months', *Washington Post*, 14 Dec 1988.
3. Quoted in Paul Warnke, 'Foreign Policy Fake, Arms Control Poseur', *New York Times*, 14 Oct 1988, p. A35.
4. Statement of Vice President George Bush, 'Defense', in *Bush for President Issue Paper*, undated, p. 4.
5. See for example Under Secretary of State Michael Armacost, 'Military Power and Diplomacy: The Reagan Legacy', in *Current Policy Paper No 1108* (Washington DC: US Department of State, 1988): 'to maintain the peace, we must preserve our strength, and, more than that, we have to be willing to use our strength'.
6. Quoted in *Newsweek*, 19 Dec 1988, p. 30.
7. Henry Kissinger, 'A Memo to the Next President', in *Newsweek*, 19 Sept 1988, p. 34.
8. Henry Kissinger and Cyrus Vance, 'Bipartisan Objectives for Foreign Policy', in *Foreign Affairs*, Summer 1988, pp. 900–10.
9. The editors, 'The Next Four Years', in *Foreign Affairs*, Winter 1988/89.
10. Ibid., p. 7.
11. Quoted from the Commission on Integrated Long-Term Strategy, *Discriminate Deterrence* (Washington DC: US Government Printing Office, Jan 1988).
12. Henry Kissinger, 'NATO: The Next Thirty Years', Brussels speech, 1 Sept 1978.
13. For a summary see Michael Lucas, 'The United States and Post-INF Europe', in *World Policy Journal*, Spring 1988, pp. 195–200.

14. Zbigniew Brzezinski, 'America's New Geostrategy', in *Foreign Affairs*, Spring 1988, p. 686.
15. Strauss quoted in Lucas, 'Post-INF Europe', p. 190.
16. Brent Scowcroft and R. James Woolsey, 'Panel Report: Defense and Arms Control', in Jimmy Carter and Gerald Ford, eds, *American Agenda, Report to the Forty-First President of the United States* (1988).
17. For the extended neo-conservative argument, see Melvin Krauss, *How NATO Weakens the West* (New York: Simon and Schuster, 1986).
18. For Schroeder's views see Committee on Armed Services, *Report of the Defense Burdensharing Panel* (Washington DC: US House of Representatives, Aug 1988).
19. Zbigniew Brzezinski, *Game Plan* (Boston: Atlantic Monthly Press, 1986); Henry Kissinger, 'A Plan to Reshape NATO', in *Time*, 5 Mar 1984, pp. 20–4.
20. 'Fewer Weapons and Troops to Fire Them', *Washington Post*, 25 Apr 1988, p. A4.
21. Estimated in David P. Calleo, *Beyond American Hegemony* (New York: Basic Books, 1987) pp. 165–6.
22. For a discussion see Calleo, *Beyond American Hegemony*.
23. Warren Christopher and Lawrence Eagleburger, 'Foreign Policy', in Ford and Carter, eds, *American Agenda*, p. 5.
24. Reagan and Shultz quoted in *Newsweek*, 19 Dec 1988, pp. 29, 31.
25. Henry Kissinger, 'Gorbachev and the West's Wishful Thinkers', in *Washington Post*, 20 Dec 1988, p. A25.
26. Sam Nunn, 'Responding to Gorbachev', in *Washington Post*, 18 Dec 1988, p. C7.
27. *Newsweek*, 19 Dec 1988, p. 25.
28. Quoted in 'Bush Pledges "Hard" Look at Soviet Plan', in *Washington Post*, 15 Dec 1988, p. A33.
29. Quoted in 'Bush Team to Seek Change in Military', in *New York Times*, 18 Dec 1988, p. A34.
30. Quoted in 'U.S. Redefines Policy on Security to Place Less Stress on Soviets', in *Wall Street Journal*, 11 Aug 1988, p. 1.

3 'New Thinking' and Soviet Strategy

1. Alan Wolfe, *The Rise and Fall of the Soviet Threat: Domestic Sources of the Cold War Consensus* (Washington DC: Institute for Policy Studies, 1979).
2. Jonathan Dean, *Watershed in Europe: Dismantling the East–West Military Confrontation* (Lexington: Lexington Books, 1987).
3. Patrick Litherland, 'Gorbachev and Arms Control: Civilian Experts and Soviet Policy', *Peace Research Report No 12*, University of Bradford, 1986.

4. Stephen Shenfield, *The Nuclear Predicament: Explorations in Soviet Ideology* (London: RIIA/Routledge & Kegan Paul, 1987).

5. Michael MccGwire, *Military Objectives in Soviet Foreign Policy* (Washington DC: The Brookings Institution, 1987).

6. Quoted in *Soviet News*, 26 Feb 1986, p. 89.

7. Institute of World Economy and International Relations, USSR Academy of Sciences, *Disarmament and Security: 1987 Yearbook* (Moscow: Novosti Press Agency Publishing House, 1988) p. 212.

8. See Michael MccGwire, 'A mutual security regime for Europe?' in *International Affairs*, Vol 65, No 3, Summer 1988; and Jack Snyder, 'The Gorbachev Revolution: A Waning of Soviet Expansionism?', in *International Security*, Vol 12, No 3, Winter 1987/8.

9. Moshe Lewin, *The Gorbachev Phenomenon: A historical interpretation* (London: Radius, 1988); Martin Walker, *The Waking Giant: The Soviet Union Under Gorbachev* (London: Michael Joseph, 1986).

10. *Defence Without the Bomb: Report of the Alternative Defence Commission* (London: Taylor & Francis, 1983).

11. DT Yazov, *Na strazhe sotsializma i mira* (Moskow: Voennoe Izdatel'stvo, 1987) pp. 32–3.

12. 'Shevardnadze addresses conference on foreign policy and diplomacy', in BBC *SWB* SU/0214, 27 July 1988, pp. A1/2–A1/5; 'Ligachev's speech to Gorkiy oblast party activists', in BBC *SWB* SU/0224, 8 Aug 1988, pp. B/1–B/5.

13. For further discussion, see Mammo Muchie and Hans van Zon, 'Soviet Foreign Policy Under Gorbachev and Revolution in the Third World: An Ideological Retreat or Refinement?', in Mary Kaldor, Gerard Holden and Richard Falk, eds, *The New Detente: Rethinking East–West Relations* (London: Verso/United Nations University, 1989).

14. Quoted in *Soviet News*, 14 Dec 1988; *Krasnaya Zvezda*, 8 Dec 1988.

15. Cf. repeated melodramatic interventions by Michael Heseltine on British TV.

16. In the words of an official announcement of his replacement by Colonel-General M.A. Moiseev.

4 New and Old Thinking in the Two Germanies

1. See the report of the Independent Commission on Disarmament and Security (Palme Commission) *Common Security*, (London: Pan Books, 1982). Also the SIPRI reader, *Policies for Common Security* (London and Philadelphia: Taylor & Francis, 1985).

2. See the defence concept of Rupert Scholz who was appointed Defence Secretary in June 1988 when his predecessor, Manfred Wörner, went to Brussels to become General Secretary of NATO. Scholz said in several

interviews that there cannot be a renunciation of modernisation of the nuclear systems until NATO has a comprehensive concept of arms control. He also stressed that the WTO continues to modernise its nuclear systems. Disarmament, he said, is the consequence of detente, not the other way around. For example, interview in *NATO Brief*, No 3/1988 – May/June (Brussels: NATO Information Service, 15 July 1988).

3. For details see Birckenbach/Rix/Wellmann/Statz, 'Transatlantic Crisis – A Framework for an Alternative West European Peace Policy?' in Mary Kaldor and Richard Falk, eds, *Dealignment: A New Foreign Policy Perspective* (Oxford: Basil Blackwell, 1987) pp. 113–42.

4. Shortly before the general elections in January 1987 the Greens published a booklet on SPD security policy: *Spd-Verteidigungspolitik. Ein halber Frieden* (Hamburg, Cologne, Bonn: Green Party, 1986).

5. See for details e.g. Wolfgang Berner, 'Reformdruck, Machtfragen und Partikularismus im osteuropäischen Vorfeld der UdSSR 1980-84', in *Berichte des Bundesinstituts für internationale und osteuropäische Studien* No 20 – 1984 (Cologne: Federal Institute of International and East-Scientific Studies, 1984). Also James McAdams's most stimulating study, *East Germany and Detente: Building Authority after the Wall* (Cambridge, Mass: Cambridge University Press, 1985).

6. For instance see A. Tolpegin, 'Realitäten und Illusionen. Zu Erich Honeckers BRD-Besuch', in *Neue Zeit* (German edition) No 38.87, pp. 4–5.

7. *Dokumente der Tagung des Politischen Beratenden Ausschusses der Teilnehmerstaaten des Warschauer Vertrages*, (Berlin: APN-Verlag, 28–9 May 1987, official translation from Moskow: Verlag der Presseagentuur Nowosti, 1987).

8. The proposal was for instance published in the official SED paper *Neues Deutschland*, 19 July 1988.

9. *Neues Deutschland*, 24 Jan 1989.

10. See for example Walter Süss, 'Kein Vorbild für die DDR? Die sowjetischen Reformbemühungen aus der Sicht der SED', in *Deutschland Archiv*, No 9/86, pp. 967–88. Also Bernard von Plate, 'Zum Profil der DDR in der sozialistischen Staatengemeinschaft' in 'Die DDR in der sozialistischen Staatengemeinschaft', (reader for conference *XX Tagung zum Stand der DDR-Forschung*, 9–12 June 1987; Cologne: Verlag Wissenschaft und Politik, 1988) p. 15.

11. For the history of the GDR see McAdams, *East Germany and Detente*.

12. 'Der Streit der Ideologien und die Gemeinsame Sicherheit', published in several West German newspapers and in *Neues Deutschland*, 28 August 1987.

13. According to the Allensbacher Institute, in Aug 1987 50 per cent of respondents said they would agree to unilateral steps. In Feb 1986 41 per cent answered 'yes' when asked if they supported unilateral steps.

5 Conventional Forces in Europe

1. See my 'Can NATO Afford a Non-suicidal Strategy?' in Gwyn Prins, ed, *The Choice: Nuclear Weapons versus Strategy* (London: Chatto and Windus, 1984).
2. Matthew Evangelista, 'Stalin's Postwar Army Reappraised', in *International Security*, Winter 1982/3, p. 111.
3. Alain C. Enthoven and K. Wayne Smith, *How Much is Enough? Shaping the Defense Program 1961–69* (New York: Harper & Row, 1971).
4. Office of the Assistant Secretary of Defense, *NATO Center Region Military Balance Study 1978–1984*, July 1979, p. 2 (declassified July 1985).
5. John Stokes, *Threat Assessment*, Report submitted to the Assembly by the Committee on Defence Questions (Paris: Western European Union, Nov 1987); Senator Carl Levin, 'Beyond the Bean Count: Realistically Assessing the Conventional Military Balance in Europe' (Washington DC: Senate Armed Services Subcommittee on Conventional Forces and Allied Defense, July 1988); James Meacham, 'A Survey of NATO's Central Front', *Economist*, 30 Aug 1986.
6. International Institute for Strategic Studies, *Military Balance 1987–1988* (London: IISS, 1987) p. 230.
7. See for example 'Pentagon Study Finds NATO's Conventional Forces Can Deter Attack', *International Herald Tribune*, 1 Dec 1987.
8. For one case study, see Malcolm Chalmers and Lutz Unterseher, 'Is there a Tank Gap? Comparing NATO and the Warsaw Pact Tank Fleets', in *International Security*, Summer 1988, pp. 5–49.
9. Carl Levin, 'Bean Count', pp. 59–64.
10. The Pentagon has estimated that NATO would have 3.6 support personnel for every soldier carrying a weapon, compared with 1.8 for the Warsaw Pact. NATO, *Center Region Military Balance Study*, p. 3.
11. NATO has 10,200 combat aircraft worldwide, compared with the Warsaw Pact's 10,900, including naval, air. IISS, *Military Balance*, p. 237.
12. US DoD, *Soviet Military Power 1988* (Washington DC: US Government Printing Office, 1988) p. 130.
13. Carl Levin, 'Bean Count', pp. 72–6.
14. 'Tank Driver could not Read Russian', *Jane's Defence Weekly*, 9 July 1988.
15. For a further discussion, see various articles in *International Security*, Spring 1988.
16. Among discussions of 'defensive defence' are: Labour Party, *Defence and Security for Britain* (London: The Labour Party, 1984); John Grin and Lutz Unterseher, *The Military Rationale of the SAS Defense Concept* (mimeo, 1988); Jonathan Dean, *Alternative Defense: Answer to NATO's Post-INF Problems?*, (mimeo, 1987); Bjorn Muller, *Non-offensive Defence*, newsletter published by the Centre of Peace and Conflict Research, University of Copenhagen.

17. 'A New European Defense', *Bulletin of the Atomic Scientists*, Sept 1988.
18. See Stephen M. Meyer, 'The Sources and Prospects of Gorbachev's New Political Thinking on Security', *International Security*, Fall 1988, pp. 124–63 for useful background.
19. John G. Roos and Benjamin F. Schemmer, 'Revolution in NATO's Conventional Defense Looms from "Competitive Strategies" Initiative', *Armed Forces Journal International*, Oct 1988, p. 116.
20. John Borawski, *From the Atlantic to the Urals: Negotiating Arms Control at the Stockholm Conference* (London: Pergamon-Brasseys, 1988).
21. See Jane Sharp, 'Conventional Arms Control in Europe: Problems and Prospects', in *SIPRI Yearbook 1988* (Oxford: Oxford University Press, 1988) pp. 322–3.
22. Ibid., pp. 326–33.
23. IISS, *Military Balance*, p. 237.
24. Dennis M. Gormley, '"Triple Zero" and Soviet Military Strategy', *Arms Control Today*, Jan/Feb 1988, pp. 17–20.
25. Robert Blackwill, 'Specific Approaches to Conventional Arms Control in Europe', *Survival*, Sept/Oct 1988, pp. 436–7.
26. Walter Stutzle, '1987 – the Turning Point?', *SIPRI Yearbook 1988*, note 50.
27. For examples of such proposals, see Jonathan Dean, 'Negotiable Force Reductions and Constraints on NATO and Warsaw Pact Forces in Europe', in S. Windass and E. Grove, eds, *Common Security in Europe 1988* (London: FIS, 1988); Stephen Flanagan and Andrew Hamilton, 'Arms Control and Stability in Europe', *Survival*, Sept/Oct 1988, pp. 460–1.
28. For further discussion of some recent proposals for confidence-building measures, see Dean, 'Negotiable Force Reductions'; Stanley Sloan and Mikaela Sawtelle, *Confidence Building Measures and Force Restraints for stabilizing East–West military relations in Europe* (Washington DC: Congressional Research Service, 1988).
29. After sharp increases in the early 1980s, both UK and US defence budgets have fallen in real terms in recent years. UK defence spending fell 8 per cent between 1984/5 and 1988/9 after an increase of 28 per cent in the previous six years (HMSO, *Autumn Statement 1988*, London: HMSO, 1988). US defence spending (budget authority) fell 8 per cent in real terms between Fiscal Years 1985 and 1988, after rising 64 per cent in the previous six years (IISS, *Military Balance*, p. 17).
30. The government of the Soviet Union admits that its published defence budget figures exclude military R&D and weapons procurement. More detailed information is promised by 1990. Stutzle, '1987', p. 12.

6 After the Treaty – Nuclear Forces in Europe

1. *Wall Street Journal*, 8 Nov 1988.
2. US Secretary of Defense, *Support of NATO Strategy in the 1990s*, 25 Jan 1988.

3. House Energy and Water Appropriations Committee (HEW), *DoD Energy and Water Appropriations FY 1989*, Part 6, p. 808.

4. HEW, *DoD Appropriations FY 1989*, Part 1, p. 111

5. Ibid.

6. Lothar Ruehl, State Secretary of the Federal Republic of Germany's Ministry of Defence, in *NATO's Sixteen Nations*, Aug 1987; and an internal memorandum from Ruehl to Mannfred Woerner, 17 Mar 1988 (author's translation).

7. Memorandum from Lothar Ruehl to Mannfred Woerner, 17 Mar 1988.

8. *Washington Post*, 28 Oct 1988.

9. *International Herald Tribune*, 11 Jan 1988.

10. NATO, *Allied Tactical Paper 33A* (Brussels: NATO Information Service, 1980) Chapter 8.

11. Strobe Talbott, 'How START Stopped', in *Foreign Affairs*, Fall 1988.

12. Stephen Meyer, 'The Sources and Prospects of Gorbachev's New Political Thinking', in *International Security*, Fall 1988.

13. Ibid.

14. HEW, *DoD Appropriations FY 1989*, Part 1, p. 1077.

15. Report of debate on 19 Nov in *vergaderjaar 1987–1988, 17 980 No 43, 10 Dec 1987* (The Hague: Tweede Kamer, 1988) pp. 1–9 (translated by John Hurt).

16. Translation (by John Hurt) of official stenographer's report of debate in the Dutch Lower House, 17 Dec 1987 (The Hague: Tweede Kamer, 1988).

17. Caspar Weinberger, *Report on the Nuclear Posture of NATO*, Annex B: 'NATO Decisions on Future Non-Strategic Nuclear Force' (Washington DC: Department of Defense, May 1984).

18. Letter from Wareing to Trefgarne, 27 Feb 1985.

19. Letter from Trefgarne to Wareing, 26 Mar 1985.

20. Letter from Thatcher to Wareing, 6 May 1987.

21. 'The Montebello Decision, 27 Oct 1983', in *NATO Final Communiques 1981-85* (Brussels: NATO Information Service, 1986) pp. 106–7.

22. Joshua Handler and William M. Arkin, 'Nuclear Weapons and Naval Nuclear Weapons: A Complete Inventory', in *Neptune Papers* No 2 (Washington DC: Greenpeace and Institute for Policy Studies, May 1988) p. 7.

23. *Statement on the Defence Estimates*, 1985 and 1988.

24. For example, *Arms Control Impact Statements FY 1984* (Washington DC: US Arms Control and Disarmament Agency, 1983) p. 185.

25. HEW, *DoD Authorization of Appropriations FY 1985*, Part 1, p. 932.

26. Thames TV, 'This Week', 10 Dec 1987.

27. *U.S. Ground Forces and the Conventional Balance in Europe*, June 1988.

28. J.M. Epstein, *Measuring Military Power, The Soviet Air Threat to Europe* (London: Taylor & Francis, 1984); Carnegie Panel on US Security, *Challenges for US National Security* Part 2, 'Assessing the Balance: Defense

Spending and Conventional Forces' (Washington DC: Carnegie Foundation, 1981) p. 71.

29. HEW, *DoD Appropriations FY 1989*, Part 1, pp. 29–30.
30. *Washington Times*, 22 Sept 1987, p. 5.
31. *Washington Times*, 17 Feb 1988.
32. *Washington Post*, 2 Mar 1988.
33. Bernard P. Randolph, USAF Deputy Chief of Staff for Research, Development and Acquisition, *DoD Appropriations FY 1988*, Part 5 (House Defense Appropriations Sub-Committee) p. 399.
34. General Kavanaugh before House Energy Appropriations FY 89, March 21 1988, p. 1121–2.
35. Given that only approximately 300 GLCM warheads were produced and that there are 24 planes in a squadron, outfitting three squadrons would mean around four missiles per plane. Assuming that this figure applies to the most capable US plane, the different versions of the F-111, and assuming that only half the force of 144 F-111s currently in the UK would be equipped with missiles and the remainder with bombs produces a figure of some 300 missiles. Including a further 50 F-111G (converted FB-111A) adds 200 (although these planes currently carry a SRAM 1). The entire F-111 force is to receive an avionics upgrade (not just the FB-111A/F-111G) so the entire force will be able to use the new systems.

Assuming that the equivalent of two tactical fighter wings of 72 F-15E are deployed to Europe, and that these carry two missiles each, adds a further 288. In addition they will be deployed with the three wings of US F-16s. If a quarter of the force is actually equipped with two missiles each this would give a figure of 110 missiles supporting the force. Only a proportion of the aircraft in nuclear-certified allied squadrons are actually equipped with nuclear weapons. Assuming that only one-sixth are so equipped, 140 missiles would be needed. These figures, 300 + 200 + 288 + 110 + 140, give a total of around 1,100 TASMs. Including a partial deployment with the UK's Tornado adds around 300.

36. *Washington Post*, 21 Sept 1988.
37. Senate Armed Services Committee, *Hearings on NATO Defense and the INF Treaty*, 2 Feb 1988, p. 178.
38. HEW, *DoD Appropriations FY 1989*, Part 7, p. 334.
39. *Defense News*, 22 Aug 1988.
40. *House Appropriations Committee*, FY 1989, Part 1, p. 30.
41. *New York Times*, 16 Dec 1987.
42. *Annual Report* of the US Secretary of Defense, FY 1989.
43. *International Defense Review*, Nov 1987; see also *Armed Forces*, Vol 6, No 2, Feb 1987.
44. Dr Robert E. Barker, Assistant to the Secretary of Defense (Atomic Energy), HEW Subcommittee, FY 1988, Part 6, p. 797.

45. *House Appropriations Committee*, FY 1989, Part 1, p. 714.
46. US Senate Energy and Water Committee, *Authorization FY 86, Atomic Energy Defense Activities*, p. 1462.
47. US Senate Armed Services Committee, *Authorization FY 1988 and 89*, Part 1, p. 66.
48. *Armed Forces*, Vol 6, No 2, Feb 1987; *Military Balance 1987-8* (London: International Institute for Strategic Studies, 1987).
49. US House of Representatives Armed Services Committee, *Authorization and Oversight FY 1985*, Part 1, p. 932.
50. *Economist*, 20 Aug 1988.

7   The Power of Star Wars

An earlier version of this chapter was originally published in the May 1988 issue of *Socialist Review*, by the Center for Social Research and Education, 3202 Adeline, Berkeley, CA 94703. The author would like to thank Mary Kaldor, who inspired the approach of the analysis, and colleagues in the 1986–7 Corliss Lamont Program at Columbia University, directed by Seymour Melman.

1. For an overview of the technological performances and strategies of the US, Western Europe and Japan, see my *New Technologies across the Atlantic: US Leadership or European Autonomy?* (Brighton: Wheatsheaf, 1988).
2. Case studies of the US policies on technology transfer, semiconductors and telecommunications are offered in my *New Technologies*. On the US Trade Bill see Peter Kilborn, 'US Trade Bill signals a Major Shift in Policy', in *International Herald Tribune*, 30 Apr 1988.
3. The militarisation of the US industry and technology has been widely documented. See in particular Ann Markusen, 'The Militarized Economy', *World Policy Journal*, Summer 1986; Seymour Melman, *Profits without Production* (New York: Knopf, 1983); John Tirman, ed, *The Militarization of High Technology* (Cambridge, Mass: Ballinger, 1984) and Mary Kaldor, *The Baroque Arsenal* (London: Deutsch, 1981). The growing 'specialisation' of the US as a military producer was shown also by 1988's decision by the Reagan Administration to increase to US $15 billion US arms sales abroad in 1988, 28 per cent more than in 1987 (Robert Pear, 'White House seeks a 28% increase in weapons sales', in *International Herald Tribune*, 3 May 1988).
4. The first critical analysis of the strategic shift in SDI is by E.P. Thompson, 'Folly's Comet', in E.P. Thompson, ed, *Star Wars* (Harmondsworth: Penguin, 1985). See also John Tirman, ed, *Empty Promise: the Growing Case*

against Star Wars (Boston: Beacon Press/Union of Concerned Scientists, 1986).

5. The technological shortcomings of SDI research have been documented by various recent studies. The official report on SDI by the Defense Science Board of the Department of Defense concluded that 'as a consequence of the current gaps in system design and key technologies, there is presently no way of assessing: 1. system performance against Joint Chiefs of Staff requirements; 2. system cost; 3. schedule'. It argued that 'funding requirements for the plans we have seen ... greatly exceed the amounts currently under discussion in the Congress ... None of the current cost estimates can be relied upon.' ('Excerpts from Defense Science Board Report on SDI', in *Arms Control Today*, July-Aug 1987, pp. 22–3.)

   In April 1987 the American Physical Society published a report by a Study Group on 'Science and Technology of Directed Energy Weapons', which later appeared in *Reviews of Modern Physics*. The Society's view: 'we estimate that even in the best of circumstances a decade or more of intensive research would be required to provide the technical knowledge needed for an informed decision about the potential effectiveness and survivability of directed energy weapons systems. In addition, the important issues of overall system integration and effectiveness depend critically upon information that, to our knowledge, does not yet exist' (p. 2).

6. Reply to the questions on nuclear policy submitted to all candidates by the Peace Commission of the Episcopal Diocese of Washington. See Charles Martin, 'Democrats Reply: the Candidates Face the Nuclear Question', in *International Herald Tribune*, 21 Apr 1988.

7. Commission on Integrated Long-term Strategy, *Discriminate Deterrence* (Washington DC: Jan 1988) pp. 2 and 54. It should be stressed that the report refers to the 'early deployment' version of strategic defence.

8. Council on Economic Priorities, *Star Wars, the Eonomic Fallout* (Cambridge, Mass: Ballinger, 1988), p. 54.

9. 'Groans of academe', in *Economist*, 15 Nov 1986, pp. 22–3. To encourage SDI research in universities and in small laboratories, SDIO set up a separate agency, 'Innovative Science and Technology' (IST), funded with 5 per cent of the total SDI budget. In 1985 IST gave $28 million to universities, in 1986 the amount rose to $100 million. $62 million have so far been assigned to six research consortia, including 29 universities in 16 states (Council on Economic Priorities, *Economic Fallout*, p. 84).

   In spite of this increasing dependence on military funds, the US academic world has remained largely opposed to Star Wars. A Cornell University survey of 451 physicists, engineers, chemists and mathematicians in the National Academy of Sciences showed that 80 per cent were opposed to SDI and only 10 per cent supported the current research programme (see F. Kaplan, '4 of 5 top US scientists oppose Star Wars, poll finds', in *Boston Globe*, 31 Oct 1986.

10. John Pike, 'Barriers to European Participation in the Strategic Defense Initiative', Statement to the Subcommittee on Economic Stabilization of the US House of Representatives, 10 Dec 1985, p. 12.

11. K. Rubin and G. Frisvold, 'Reagan's New Economic Agenda', in *Capital and Class*, Summer 1985, p. 7. The rise in military industry's profits has closely followed the acceleration of the arms race. The General Accounting Office has reported that 'defense contractors were 35 percent more profitable than commercial manufacturers during 1970–79 and 120 percent more profitable during 1980–83'. (Quoted in M. Clayton 'Foɪ contractors a retreat but not a rout in Pentagon spending', in *Christian Science Monitor*, 12 Jan 1987.

12. Quoted in Council on Economic Priorities, *Economic Fallout*, p. 44.

13. Quoted in Council on Economic Priorities, *Economic Fallout*, pp. 98–106.

14. Quoted in Council on Economic Priorities, *Economic Fallout*, p. 95.

15. Quoted in Council on Economic Priorities, *Economic Fallout*, p. 128.

16. Quoted in Council on Economic Priorities, *Economic Fallout*, p. 131.

17. Quoted in Council on Economic Priorities, *Economic Fallout*, p. 142.

18. Nathan Rosenberg, *Civilian 'Spillovers' from Military R&D Spending: the American Experience since World War II* (Stanford University, Sept 1986, p. 30).

19. Rosenberg, *Spillovers*, pp. 30–2.

20. W. Zegveld and C. Enzing, *SDI and Industrial Technology Policy: Threat or Opportunity?* (New York: St Martin's Press, 1987), p. 177; Markusen, 'Militarized Economy', p. 506; Council for Science and Society, *UK Military R&D* (Oxford: Oxford University Press, 1986) p. 46; E. Skons, 'The SDI Program and International Research Cooperation', in SIPRI Yearbook 1986, *World Armament and Disarmament* (London: Taylor & Francis, 1986), p. 282.

A further revealing insight into the contradictions between SDI, the existing technological 'style' of the US military, and industrial production systems is offered by a congressional report to senator Proxmire on SDI progress. The study noted that 'in order to make the tens of thousands of SDI missiles and satellites affordable, SDI officials say that "Henry Ford production methods" will have to be introduced into the way these vehicles are produced. The aerospace and defense industry will have to undergo fundamental changes in their methods of production so a missile will cost hundreds of thousands of dollars instead of millions, and a satellite will cost millions of dollars instead of hundreds of millions' (D. Waller et al., *SDI: Progress and Challenges*, Staff report submitted to Senator William Proxmire, Senator J. Bennett Johnston and Senator Lawton Chiles, US Senate, 17 March 1986, p. 53).

It is doubtful whether such a 'high-tech military Fordism' could solve the problems of mass production of space weapons, and it is even more unlikely that such an industrial 'model' could be of value for civilian industry.

21. A study of US, European and Japanese programmes in advanced technology is developed in my 'High Technology Programs: for the Military or for the Economy?', in *Bulletin of Peace Proposals*, Vol 19, No 1, 1988.

22. John Pike, 'Barriers'; 'Groans of Academe' *Economist*; Mark Schapiro, 'The Selling of Star Wars to Europe', in *New Statesman*, 22 Jan 1988, p. 18.

23. Peter Marsch, 'Industry failing to make most of Star wars deals', in *Financial Times*, 3 March 1988; 'Groans of Academe', *Economist*; J. Cushman, 'Europeans given U.S. missile-defense contracts', in *New York Times*, 5 Dec 1986.

24. See Michael Lucas, 'SDI and Europe', in *World Policy Journal* No 1, Spring 1986.

25. Eureka and the Human Frontiers Science Program are investigated in my 'High Technology Programs'.

26. W. Finan et al., *The US Trade Position in High Technology, 1980–1986*, Report to the Joint Economic Committee, Washington DC, 1986.

8 Looking Southwards

The author would like to thank Ellen Fichtner, who translated this chapter from the Spanish, and the following for helping obtain information: Malcolm Spaven of Sussex University's Armaments and Disarmament Information Unit; Fabrizio Battistelli of *Archivio Disarmo*, Rome; Marco de Andreis and Laura Guazzone of *Istituto di Recerche per il Disarmo, lo Sviluppo e la Pace*, Rome; and Joseph Gerson and Bruce Birchard of the American Friends Service Committee, Boston, MA.

1. Tom Frinking, 'Interim Report of the Sub-Committee on the Southern Region', North Atlantic Assembly, Document AA 198, PC/SR (83) 7, Nov 1983.

2. Quoted in *Guardian*, 15 June 1986.

3. Quoted in William M. Arkin, 'A Global Role for NATO' in *Bulletin of Atomic Scientists*, Jan 1986.

4. George Schultz, 'Low-Intensity Warfare: The Challenge of Ambiguity', address to the Low-Intensity Warfare Conference, Washington DC, National Defense University, 15 Jan 1986.

5. Quoted in *New York Times*, 30 Jan 1980.

6. For a detailed study about the debate on 'out-of-area' operations, see Charles A. Kupchan, *The Persian Gulf and the West: the Dilemmas of Security* (London: Allen & Unwin, 1987) p. 177ff.

7. Quoted in Miguel Herrero Rodríguez de Miñón, *Final Report of the Sub-Committee on Out-of-Area Security Challenges to the Alliance*, North Atlantic Assembly, Document AD 81 PC/OA (86) 1, May 1986, p. 39. Other important alliance reports are taken from the same source. (Rodríguez de Miñón is the MP representing *Alianza Popular*, the most important party of the Spanish right).

8. NATO Information Service, *La Alianza Atlántica*, (Brussels: 1984, Spanish version) p. 309.

9. Kupchan, *The Persian Gulf*, p. 164.

10. NATO Defence Planning Committee, Brussels, May 1980.

11. NATO Defence Planning Committee, Brussels, May 1981.

12. North Atlantic Council, June 1982.

13. NATO Defence Planning Committee, Brussels, December 1982 (author's emphasis).

14. David Dimbleby and David Reynolds, *An Ocean Apart* (London: Hodder & Stoughton, 1988) pp. 312–15.

15. NATO Defence Planning Committee, Brussels, June 1983; US Congress, *House Appropriations Committee, Military Construction Appropriations for 1983*, Part 5 (Washington DC: Government Printing Office, 1982) p. 257.

16. Quoted in *Le Monde*, 10 Feb 1984.

17. Paul E. Gallis, *The NATO Allies, Japan and the Persian Gulf*, Congressional Research Service, Report No 84-184F, 8 Nov 1984, p. 43.

18. Gallis, *The Nato Allies*, p. 37.

19. For more on the attack on Libya, see Mary Kaldor and Paul Anderson, eds, *Mad Dogs: The US Raids on Libya* (London: Pluto Press, 1986); Bob Woodward, *Veil: The Secret Wars of the CIA* (New York: Simon & Schuster, 1987); *International Herald Tribune*, 12 Jan 1988; and Mariano Aguirre and Robert Matthews, *Doctrina Reagan y Guerras de Baja Intensidad* (forthcoming in Spain, 1989).

20. Theodore Draper, 'American Hubris: From Truman to the Persian Gulf', in *New York Review of Books*, 16 July 1987, p. 44.

21. *International Herald Tribune*, 8 Oct 1987.

22. According to the *Washington Post* the US naval buildup reached a peak of 48 ships, but the paper does not indicate a date for this figure (*International Herald Tribune*, 12 Jan 1988) and *El País*, 30 June 1987).

23. Joseph Fitchett, 'Gulf Armada Seen as a Quiet Plus for West', *International Herald Tribune*, 18 Nov 1987. A detailed list of the US and European presence in the Gulf at the end of 1987 is in 'Situation Report: US and European Forces in the Persian Gulf', in *Fact Sheet*, Center for Defense Information, 9 Mar 1988. The data from other sources vary slightly and depend on the dates.

24. 'A Further Note on US Military Options in the Gulf', in *Peace Studies Briefing*, No 35, University of Bradford: School of Peace Studies, 10 Sept 1987, p. 5.

25. Rodríguez de Miñón, *Final Report*, p. 15.
26. Marc Betinck, 'NATO's Out-of-Area Problem', in *Adelphi Papers*, No 211, Autumn 1986, p. 28. For another example of global analysis on NATO tasks, see Lord Home of the Hirsel, 'North Atlantic to South Pacific: A World Brief for NATO', in *The Times*, 11 Apr 1984.
27. Rodríguez de Miñón, *Final Report*, p. 15.
28. Rodríguez de Miñón, *Final Report*, p. 22.
29. Rodríguez de Miñón, *Final Report*, p. 23.
30. Helmoed-Romer Heitman, 'The South Atlantic. NATO's Unprotected Communications Zone', in *Navy International*, Feb 1985, pp. 103–7. See also John Chipman, 'NATO and Out-of-Area Insecurity', in *Estratégia* No 3, 1987, Lisbon Instituto de Estudos Estratégicos e Internacionais, p. 133.
31. Helen Kitchen, 'Africa' in Robert H. Kupperman and William J. Taylor, Jr, eds, *Strategic Requirements for the Army to the Year 2000* (Lexington: Lexington Books/The Center for Strategic and International Studies, 1984) pp. 486–7.
32. Heitman, 'The South Atlantic'; and Contralmirante Salgado Alba, 'Análisis Estratégico del Atlántico Sur', in *Estratégia*, No 3, p. 155.
33. Daniel Fitz-Simons, 'Central America and its Strategic Importance to NATO', paper for the Council for Inter-American Security, Washington DC, 1986.
34. James R. Greene and Brent Scowcroft, eds, *Intereses Occidentales y Política de Estados Unidos en el Caribe. Informe del Grupo de Trabajo del Consejo Atlántico sobre la Cuenca del Caribe* (Buenos Aires: Grupo Editor Latino-americano, 1985) p. 21. (First published as *Western Interests and US Policy Options in the Caribbean Basin* (Boston: The Atlantic Council, Oelgesch-lager, Gunn & Hain Publishers, Inc.).
35. Greene and Scowcroft, *Intereses*, p. 50.
36. Rodríguez de Miñón, *Final Report*, p. 22.
37. Henry Kissinger, *Years of Upheaval* (London: Weidenfield & Nicolson and Michael Joseph, 1982) p. 713.
38. *International Herald Tribune*, 1 June 1984.
39. Quoted in Gallis, *The NATO Allies*, p. 34.
40. For more on the question of Soviet expansionism in the Third World, see Bentinck, 'NATO's Out-of-Area Problems', pp. 30, 34–5, 39–41; Samuel F. Wells and Mark Bruzonsky, eds, *Security in the Middle East* (Boulder: West-view, 1987) p. 9 and Chapters 12 and 13; Thomas L. McNaugher, *Arms and Oil* (Washington DC: The Brookings Institution, 1985) pp. 45–6; Paul Kennedy, *The Rise and Fall of the Great Powers* (London: Unwin Hyman, 1986) pp. 511–12.
41. Nicolas Mosar, *Interim Report of the Sub-Committee on Out-of-Area Security Challenges to the Alliance*, North Atlantic Assembly, Document AA 200 PC/OA (83,7), Brussels: November 1983, p. 4.

42. Lawrence Eagleburger, 'The Transatlantic Relationship – A Long Term Perspective', *NATO Review*, April 1984, pp. 8–14.

43. See James R. Blaker, 'The Out-of-Area Question and NATO Burden Sharing' in Linda P. Brady and Joyce P. Kaufman, eds, *NATO in the 1980s* (New York: Praeger, 1985) p. 39ff; Committee on Armed Services, House of Representatives, *Report of the Defense Burdensharing Panel* (Washington DC: US Government Printing Office, 1988).

44. Eurogroup, *Western Defence: The European Role in NATO*, Brussels: May 1988, pp. 16–17.

45. House Appropriations Committee, *Military Construction Appropriations for 1984*, Part 5.

46. Kupchan, *The Persian Gulf*, p. 193ff.

47. Charles Goerens, 'El Porvenir de la Unión Europea Occidental', in *Revista Española de Defensa*, No 8, Oct 1988, p. 81.

48. Geoffrey Kemp, 'Time for a British-Style Review of Commitments', in *International Herald Tribune*, 23 Nov 1987. See also: Committee on Defence Questions and Armaments, Assembly of Western European Union, *Burden Sharing in the Alliance*, Document 947, Paris: WEU, 18 May 1983.

49. Andrew McEwen, 'Europe Moves Towards Gulf Role', in *The Times*, 3 Sept 1987.

50. Frinking, *Interim Report*, p. 25.

51. Lieutenant-General James M. Thompson, 'The Southern Flank and Out-of-Area Operations', RUSI 128 No 4, Dec 1983, p. 15.

52. About the Soviet danger in the Third World see Sergio A. Rossi, 'NATO's Southern Flank and Mediterranean Security' in H.F. Zeiner-Gunersen et al., *NATO's Maritime Flanks: Problems and Prospects* (Washington DC: Institute for Foreign Policy Analysis/Pergamon-Brassey's, 1987) p. 49ff.

53. Among the ample bibliography on this subject, see André Glucksmann, *La Fuerza del Vértigo* (Barcelona: Planeta, 1986); Alain Finkielkraut, *La Derrota del Pensamiento* (Barcelona: Anagrama, 1987).

54. Claude Nigoul and Maurice Torrelli, *Menaces en Méditerranée* (Paris: Fondation pour les Etudes de Défense Nationale, 1987) p. 27.

55. Nigoul and Torrelli, *Menaces*, p. 14. See also Pierre Lellouche, 'A Threat to Europe's Future', in *Newsweek*, 31 Oct 1988.

56. Nigoul and Torrelli, *Menaces*, p. 233ff.

57. Admiral Harry Train, 'Maritime Strategy in the Mediterranean', in *Adelphi Papers*, No 229, Spring 1988, p. 49.

58. John Chipman, 'NATO and the Security Problems of the Southern Region: From Azores to Ardahan' in John Chipman, ed, *NATO's Southern Allies: Internal and External Challenges* (London: Routledge & Kegan Paul, 1988) p. 30.

59. William M. Arkin, 'The Nuclear Arms Race at Sea', in *Neptune Papers*, No 1

(Washington DC: Institute for Policy Studies/Greenpeace, Oct 1987) pp. 10–11; Malcolm Dando, 'NATO's Maritime Strategy: the Sea Route to Nuclear War', in *Sanity*, June 1987, p. 26.

60. Maurice Cremazco, 'The Military Presence of the Riparian Countries' in G. Luciani, ed, *The Mediterranean Region* (London: Croom Helm, 1984) pp. 210–12; Vicenç Fisas Armengol, *Paz en el Mediterráneo*, (Barcelona: Lerna, 1987).

61. Chipman, 'NATO and Security Problems', p. 43.

62. Kupperman and Taylor, *Strategic Requirement*, p. 134.

63. Alvaro Vasconcelos, 'Portuguese Defence Policy: Internal Politics and Defence Commitments' in Chipman, ed, *NATO's Southern Allies*, p. 115.

64. Congressional Research Service, *US Military Installations in NATO's Southern Region*, Report to the Subcommittee on Europe and the Middle East of the Committee on Foreign Affairs, US House of Representatives (Washington DC: Government Printing Office, 7 Oct 1986) p. 59.

65. *International Herald Tribune*, 2 May 1987.

66. *Jane's Defence Weekly*, 18 Apr 1987, p. 687.

67. US Senate, *Military Construction Appropriation Bill*, 1988, p. 13.

68. *International Herald Tribune*, 25 Jan 1988.

69. Television interview with Chancellor Helmut Schmidt, quoted in Robert J. Lieber, 'Middle East Oil and the Industrial Democracies: Conflict and Cooperation in the Aftermath of the Oil Shocks', in Wells and Bruzonsky, eds, *Security*, p. 230. On the international division of labour within the alliance, see Amitav Achrya, 'NATO and Out-Of-Area' Contingencies. The Gulf Experience', in *International Defence Review*, May 1987, p. 572. See also the Commission on Integrated Long-Term Strategy, *Discriminate Deterrence* (Washington DC: Government Printing Office, Jan 1988).

70. Walter De Bock and Jean-Charles Deniau, *Des Armes Pour L'Iran* (Paris: Gallimard, 1987) p. 14.

71. For more about new conceptions of security, see Arthur Westing, 'An Expanded Concept of International Security' in Arthur Westing, ed, *Global Resources and International Conflict* (Oxford: Oxford University Press/SIPRI, 1986) p. 183ff.

72. For an evaluation of the military and economic costs of US intervention in Iran, see Michael T. Klare, *Beyond the 'Vietnam Syndrome': US Interventionism in the 1980s* (Washington DC: Institute for Policy Studies, 1981) p. 45ff. See also George Keenan in *New York Times*, 1 Feb 1980.

73. Roberto Centeno, *El Petróleo y la Crisis Mundial* (Madrid: Alianza, 1982) p. 469ff; Robin Clarke, 'Environment and Resources: Is Earth Over-Exploited?' in Isaac Asimov, ed, *Living in the Future* (London: Multimedia Publications, 1985).

74. Cynthia Pollock Shea, 'Shifting to Renewable Energy' and Christopher

Flavin and Alan Durning, 'Raising Energy Efficiency', in *State of the World 1988* (New York: Worldwatch Institute/W.W. Norton, 1988) pp. 57, 82.

75. Kupchan, *The Persian Gulf*, p. 197.

Index